HOW TO PASS

In full COLOUR

STANDARD GRADE

FRENCH

Douglas Angus

HODDER GIBSON
AN HACHETTE UK COMPANY

D0316063

Acknowledgements

The Publishers would like to thank the following for permission to reproduce copyright material:

Extracts from the GRC are reprinted by permission of the Scottish Qualifications Authority.

Original artworks by Kate Sardella, IFA Design Ltd.; additional colouring by Redmoor Design.

Cartoons © Moira Munro 2008

CD Acknowledgements

Voices: Rémy Allard, Samuel Beugné, Fanny Chouc and Anne-Hélène Sévêque.

Audio Engineering – Phil Booth, Heriot-Watt University

Every effort has been made to trace all copyright holders, but if any have been inadvertently overlooked the Publishers will be pleased to make the necessary arrangements at the first opportunity.

If the CD is missing from this package, please contact us on 0141 848 1609 or at hoddergibson@hodder.co.uk, advising where and when you purchased the book.

Although every effort has been made to ensure that website addresses are correct at time of going to press, Hodder Gibson cannot be held responsible for the content of any website mentioned in this book. It is sometimes possible to find a relocated web page by typing in the address of the home page for a website in the URL window of your browser.

Hachette's policy is to use papers that are natural, renewable and recyclable products and made from wood grown in sustainable forests. The logging and manufacturing processes are expected to conform to the environment regulations of the country of origin.

Orders: please contact Bookpoint Ltd, 130 Milton Park, Abingdon, Oxon OX14 4SB. Telephone: (44) 01235 827720. Fax: (44) 01235 400454. Lines are open from 9.00–5.00, Monday to Saturday, with a 24-hour message answering service. Visit our website at www.hoddereducation.co.uk. Hodder Gibson can be contacted direct on: Tel: 0141 848 1609; Fax: 0141 889 6315; email: hoddergibson@hodder.co.uk

© Douglas Angus 2005, 2008
First published in 2005 by
Hodder Gibson, an imprint of Hodder Education
an Hachette UK company
2a Christie Street
Paisley PA1 1NB

This colour edition first published 2008

Impression number	5 4 3 2
Year	2012 2011 2010

Cover photo © Peter Adams (ba01261)
Typeset in 10.5 on 14pt Frutiger Light by Phoenix Photosetting, Chatham, Kent
Printed and bound in Italy.

A catalogue record for this title is available from the British Library

ISBN-13: 978 0 340 97390 5

CONTENTS

Chapter 1   Introduction 1

Chapter 2   Reading 8

Chapter 3   Reading: Foundation and General Levels 13

Chapter 4   Reading: Credit Level 18

Chapter 5   Answers to the Reading Tests 24

Chapter 6   Listening 26

Chapter 7   Listening: Foundation and General Levels 28

Chapter 8   Listening: Credit Level 39

Chapter 9   Transcripts and answers to the Listening Tests 42

Chapter 10 Speaking 56

Chapter 11 Writing 72

Chapter 12 Structures and vocabulary 79

INTRODUCTION

This book is a guide to the four skill areas of Standard Grade French, and to how to get the best possible mark in each area: reading, listening, speaking and writing. For reading and listening, there are also practice questions, with answers so that you can check your work. For speaking and writing, we work through some sample questions, looking at how to improve your performance in assessments. The accompanying CD-ROM contains listening material, to be used with the questions and tapescripts in the book. (These are indicated in the book by the ⊙ symbol.)

What is the exam like?

Standard Grade French will test you on four skills: reading, listening, speaking and writing. Two of the skills, reading and listening, will be assessed at the end of the course in an external exam set by SQA (Scottish Qualifications Authority). The other two skills, speaking and writing, will be assessed differently. Speaking is carried out in three tests set and marked by your teacher: the marks for the three tests will be added together to give you a final speaking mark. For writing, you will produce over the year three pieces of writing under exam conditions, which will be collected by your teacher as a folio of writing and sent off to SQA to be marked. In this book, you will find a chapter to help you work on and revise each skill.

How is my final mark made up?

You need to be good at maths to work this one out! You will be given a grade for each of the four skills: speaking and reading will be double-weighted in the calculation of your overall award for French. This means:

◆ **Reading:** the mark you get in the final exam will be doubled.

◆ **Listening:** the mark you get in the final exam will be added to this.

◆ **Writing:** the marks you get for your three pieces of writing will be added up, and then divided by three to give a writing grade: this average grade will be added to the listening and reading grades.

◆ **Speaking:** the marks you get for your three speaking assessments will be added up and divided by three to give you a grade for speaking: this will be doubled and added to the other three grades.

◆ **Total:** you now have a total mark, which will be divided by six to give your overall grade.

What do I have to know?

You will need to know basic vocabulary covering a list of topic areas, which can be found in Chapter 12. This will help you listen and read French more easily. It will also help you to produce your own written and spoken French. You will find lists of useful vocabulary with each of the speaking and writing preparation tasks, as well as with the listening tasks.

You will need to know the basics of grammar, so that you can write and speak French correctly. The basics are in a table on pages 6 and 7, and there is further work on this area in the speaking and writing chapters.

You must be able to use a dictionary, to help you understand French in the reading exam, and to let you find words you need for your speaking and writing.

What exactly is involved in the exam?

Speaking

Speaking will be assessed by your teacher and externally moderated (checked) by SQA. Assessment tasks will arise out of your normal classwork.

You will have to carry out three tasks:

◆ a prepared talk on a topic you choose (using no more than five headings of up to eight words each in English, or in French);

◆ a conversation (on the same or a different topic);

◆ role-play requiring polite language (this means you have to use *vous,* not *tu*).

You should be able to demonstrate the ability to take part in a conversation, to use polite language as appropriate and be able to cope with additional questions or problems.

Grades will be awarded for your performance in each of the three types of task. Final grades will be awarded by working out the average of the three grades. Final grades containing ·66 should be rounded up. Final grades containing ·33 should be rounded down.

Listening

Listening will be assessed by an external examination. There will be two separate papers, one at each level. You will hear the French three times.

Questions will be set and answered in English, and they may be multiple-choice or gap-filling tasks, even at Credit level.

You will **not** be allowed to use a French–English dictionary.

Reading

Reading will also be assessed by an external examination. There will be two separate papers, one at each level; each paper will include several texts.

Questions will be set and answered in English, including multiple-choice or gap-filling tasks.

Unusual words will be translated for you in a glossary.

At least one passage in each paper will be vocational or work related.

You will be allowed to use a French dictionary.

The Reading paper will last 45 minutes at Foundation and General levels and one hour at Credit level.

Writing

Writing will be assessed by means of a folio of three pieces of work which will come from your normal class activities. You may select the topics, or do something that your teacher suggests. You can work from headings in either French or English. Your writing can be prepared in advance, drafted and redrafted. The final pieces must, however, be produced under controlled conditions, i.e. each piece will be written in class, within 30 minutes, under supervision, and you will not be allowed to use notes or refer to a book other than a dictionary.

Pieces of writing should normally be between 25 and 200 words in length, should relate to three different topics or tasks and should be your best work.

All writing tests will be marked externally by SQA.

Basic grammar

When marking your work, teachers will be looking for accuracy in basic structures. This is straightforward, simple language, and you should be able to show you can do at least the following things:

Verbs

◆ use the correct form of the present tense to express being, having, going, doing, liking and other activities which can be expressed using regular verb patterns in the first and third persons singular. This includes using subject pronouns (like *je, il, elle*) and correct verb endings, matching the subject;

◆ use *ne ... pas, ne ... jamais*, etc.;

◆ ask simple questions correctly;

◆ use verbs fairly accurately in personal language and polite language. This includes the correct polite verb forms, for requests (*voulez vous ..., je voudrais ...*) and also includes the correct verb forms for plural subjects: *mes sœurs ont ..., mes amis sont ....*

Nouns
- ◆ use the correct type of article/determiner (a, the, this), and, if you can, the correct form (e.g. correct gender or number);
- ◆ use nouns with the correct gender form of article and adjective;
- ◆ use the words for *my* and *your* correctly;

For better grades, you will have to do more than this: the grammar grid on page 5 shows what markers are going to be looking for. When you are working through the writing and speaking chapters, we will refer you to these pages sometimes, so that you can show off your knowledge of French to the examiner!

How do I go about learning vocabulary?

The best way to revise is to practise, although different people have different ways of learning vocabulary; the following ways might be useful to you.

1. Try writing out a list of words, then reading them out: cover up the French, and see if you can remember it from the English, and of course the other way round.

2. Read things over several times, on different occasions.

3. Check your memorising, by either covering one part and remembering the other, or by getting someone to do it with you (a friend or a parent). If you have someone who will help you, get them to say a word in English, which you will have to put into French.

4. Try to get your words organised into areas, so they all hang together and make sense to you.

5. Use spidergrams of related words.

Grammar grid for productive language (Speaking and Writing)

	Foundation	General	Credit
Word order	Shows awareness of different linguistic conventions, e.g. noun/adjective order	Shows some control of different linguistic conventions in straightforward expressions, e.g. position of verbs	Has control of different linguistic conventions in straightforward expressions and shows some control in more complex structures
Person	Can make person understood	Uses subject pronouns/verb endings (as appropriate) fairly consistently and shows awareness of the use of object pronouns	Uses subject and object pronouns consistently and shows awareness of the use of indirect object pronouns
Tense and mood	Can use high-frequency verbs in present tense with some accuracy in first and third persons singular	Can use present tense and at least one other with some accuracy in all persons	Can use a range of tenses as appropriate
	Can articulate basic questions to adults and peers	Can articulate common questions using politeness conventions on more demanding topics and can use common commands	Can ask a range of questions in different ways and can articulate commands
	Can use fixed phrases, e.g. I would like, I must	Can use modal verbs + infinitive in plain and polite forms (e.g. present and conditional)	Can use modal verbs + infinitive in a range of tenses as appropriate
Articles	Uses some form of article/determiner	Uses articles/determiners correctly, but may not be entirely accurate	Uses articles/determiners consistently and accurately
Cases and agreement	Shows awareness of case	Uses correct case with high-frequency expressions	Shows some control of cases (as appropriate in the language)
	Shows awareness of adjective agreement	Uses correct adjective agreement with high-frequency nouns (regular forms)	Uses correct adjective agreement with a wider range of nouns (regular and some irregular forms)

The topics you will be expected to know about will be the same for all four skills, and the SQA has given the following list from which to work. These are the areas in which you should know vocabulary to help you to cope with the listening tests, where you will not have a dictionary, and also to give you the basic vocabulary for reading tests, so you do not have to keep consulting a dictionary. There are vocabulary lists in Chapter 12 for each of these areas.

Basic topics	Standard Grade topic development
◆ name, age, where you live, nationality, points of the compass, spelling, distances	◆ personal information given/asked for in polite language
◆ members of family, friends, physical description	◆ members of family, friends and friendship, physical and character description, interpersonal problems and relationships
◆ parts of body, illness/accidents	◆ parts of body, illness/accidents, making appointments
◆ own house/rooms	◆ houses/rooms and ideal house
◆ routine	◆ comparison of routine and lifestyles in Scotland and in France/other countries
◆ birthdays, days, dates	◆ life in future, past and future events (in routine)
◆ school subjects, time	◆ comparison of Scottish system with that of France
◆ leisure, sports	◆ leisure, sports and health issues: healthy eating, exercise, drugs, TV, film and music
◆ foods/drinks	◆ other food issues, snack food, restaurants/menus, making arrangements
◆ simple directions	◆ giving simple and complex directions
◆ buildings	◆ tourist information, comparison of town/country, helping the environment
◆ pocket money	◆ changing money
◆ simple transactions	◆ e.g. souvenirs, gifts, clothes, accommodation, snacks, transport, dealing with problems in transactions
◆ jobs/working and studying	◆ relative merits of jobs, work experience, future employment

- ◆ countries/place
- ◆ travel information, travel plans, relative merits of different means of transport, comparisons between different countries
- ◆ weather
- ◆ future holidays, ideal holidays, past holidays

READING

Reading is worth **one-third** of your overall Standard Grade result: it will be tested in an external exam. The test at Foundation and General levels will last 45 minutes, and at Credit level will last 60 minutes. You will be allowed to use a dictionary for this exam, so you need to be very confident about your dictionary-use. Make sure you look at the guide to using the dictionary at the beginning of the dictionary, before you start answering questions, especially if you ever find a dictionary annoying!

The key to this assessment is finding the correct answer, and missing out the bits you do not need. Reading is a skill, and a skill you need to work on to allow you to give of your best in the final exam. The way to succeed is to extract from the text what you actually need for your answers, and to ignore the rest: the exam will test your ability to extract relevant information from the text. That means there is a lot of material which is irrelevant, and which you do not need. The skill you have to develop is the skill of identifying which bits you actually need.

There is a suggested sequence for you to follow:

1. Read the information in English about the text at the start: this should give you clues as to what the answers are going to be about. Keep this information in your head as you answer the questions!

2. Now look at the questions: this should tell you where to look in the passage for your answers. Look for clue words in the question which will show you where the answer is to be found.

3. Only now should you look at the text: skim through it to get an idea of what it is about, without using a dictionary!

4. Now look for the key areas that match your questions, and start looking for the answers just there. Remember the questions will follow the same order as the text, and you should not have to jump around all over the place.

Let us look at a couple of actual questions from past Standard Grade exams, and see how this would work in practice.

The first one is a General Reading question.

In a newspaper, you read about an accident involving a young boy.

Accident de voiture

En Charente, un garçon de quatorze ans a volé la voiture de sa mère. Après quelques minutes, il a perdu contrôle et a renversé la voiture. Résultat: des fractures au bras et à la jambe, et deux semaines à l'hôpital.

(a) What did the boy steal?   **1**

(b) Say what happened next. Mention any **three** things.   **3**

1. From the questions and the heading, you know that this is about a young boy and an accident. Skimming through the text should let you know there is a car involved, as well as a hospital.

2. The first question lets you know that he stole something, and from the text this must be *la voiture de sa mère,* as *volé* is the verb here, and it means 'steal'. You might have had to look up *volé,* but that should be all. You should be able to work out that it was his mother's car. A good tip is to use the dictionary the other way: if there is an important clue word in the question, like 'steal', and you do not know what this is in French, look it up! This will help you find where your answer is.

3. You are asked what happened next: the time phrase *Après quelques minutes* lets you know where to look. Now look for any verbs, as they will tell you what happened. You will find *perdu* and *renversé.* Remember to look for infinitives in the dictionary if you don't know the verbs, and you should find *perdre* and *renverser.* You should now be able to work out that he lost control and the car turned over. You might have to look a bit harder in the entry for *renverser* to find the correct translation, but actually it is quite obvious if you remember the context.

4. You were asked to find **three** things that happened, so if you look at the end, *deux semaines à l'hôpital,* you should have the third part.

The next example is from a Credit paper.

In a magazine, you read an article about the town of Dreux.

À minuit, au lit!

À minuit, on doit rentrer se coucher! C'est ce qu'a décidé Gérard Hamel, le maire de Dreux, pour les enfants de moins de douze ans.

Pendant tout l'été, les moins de douze ans n'ont pas le droit d'être dans la rue, entre minuit et six heures du matin, s'ils ne sont pas accompagnés d'un adulte. C'est pour protéger les jeunes enfants de tous les dangers de la rue, la nuit, explique le maire. Mais il ne veut pas arrêter là. À l'automne, il voudrait priver les parents de leurs *aides sociales s'ils ne surveillent pas leurs enfants.

Dreux est une ville qui est très touchée par le chômage. On connaît des problèmes comme les vols et les agressions. Mais interdire aux plus jeunes d'être dans la rue après minuit, est-ce que cela serait une solution?

*aides sociales – *social security payments*

(a) The mayor of Dreux has decided to introduce a curfew for children. Give any **three** details of the scheme.   3

(b) Why has he decided to take this action?   1

(c) How does he intend to penalise parents who do not supervise their children?   1

(d) Mention any **two** social problems which exist in Dreux.   2

For question (a), by looking at the first paragraph, words like *décidé*, *maire* and *enfants* show you that this is an introduction. So you should look for answers after this. The sentence *Pendant tout l'été, les moins de douze ans n'ont pas le droit d'être dans la rue, entre minuit et six heures du matin, s'ils ne sont pas accompagnés d'un adulte,* is where you should start looking, and you should see if you can find three details. First thing to look for is the verbs: *n'ont pas* and *ne sont pas accompagnés* are the two in this sentence. *They have not* and *they are not accompanied.* Your next question is: who? *Les moins de douze ans* tells you 12-year-olds: you might look up *moins*, which means 'less': remembering the context, you should work out 'children that are less than 12 years old'. You should also be able to identify *adulte*, to work out *not accompanied by an adult.* The next question is what: *They have not* what? *Le droit.* Look it up in the dictionary and you will find *law* and also *right.* Immediately after comes *to be in the street.* This should let you work out a second part of the three marks. You should also be able to work out times, for a third mark, and the season, for a fourth mark. So, for three marks, any three of these:

◆ *during the summer*

◆ *under-12 year olds don't have the right to be in the street*

◆ *between midnight and 6 a.m.*

◆ *when not accompanied by an adult*

Question (b) follows on: *explique le maire* (the mayor explains) shows you that this is the answer: again, look for the verb first: *protéger*. If you don't know it, look it up: *protect*. Looking at the rest of the sentence, it should be clear that it is

◆ *to protect children from the dangers of the street*

To answer question (c), look for parents and supervise: when you find them, you will also find a phrase which is translated in the glossary: you now need to look for the verb, which is *priver*. If you don't know it, look it up: *deprive*. Put together all the words you know, and you should come up with: *deprive the parents of their social security payments*, which you should make more meaningful:

◆ *take away from the parents their social security payments*

Question (d) asks you for social problems, **things**: for this question, you don't look for verbs, but for nouns. We can find in the next piece of text: *le chômage, les vols et les agressions*. If you don't know the words, look them up, to get two words (that is all you need):

◆ *unemployment*

◆ *thefts*

◆ *attacks/violence*

Remember, only look up what you have to: know where to look for the answer, and know what you are looking for. Verbs and nouns are the two most important things.

The other major skill needed for Reading exams is using a dictionary: it is very easy to spend far too long looking up words, and also very easy to find the wrong answer. What is worse, sometimes you cannot find an answer! It is usual to blame the dictionary for this, but more often than not it is the person looking up the dictionary who has got it wrong. Make sure you know your alphabet properly, and practise using the dictionary. When you do use it, remember the following things:

◆ When you find a word, the next thing after in many dictionaries is often the guide to pronouncing it! It might also be a word like *pret.*, which is the dictionary's way of telling you that the word you are looking up is a past tense; or *prep.*, which is telling you it is a preposition.

◆ There will often be several entries for a word, because some words are both verb and noun, with different meanings.

◆ Because French verbs have endings, you will often not find exactly the word you are looking for: you need the infinitive.

◆ Don't just look at the start of the entry, go on down the entry to see if something further down makes sense.

◆ Always keep in mind the context of the passage you are reading: that may well help you find the correct phrase in a dictionary.

◆ Watch for the little bracketed words in some dictionaries, like *(sport),* which tell you what context the word is used in.

◆ Remember, sometimes it makes sense to look up words in the English half of the dictionary, to give you a clue as to where to look for the answer to a question.

If the answer asks for two things, just give two things. The examiner will only give you marks for the first two things you write down, and you will get no credit for something that is correct, but given later on in the answer, if there is a wrong answer given before it.

Vocabulary tips

There are some vocabulary areas which always come up in the exam, and it is important that you know and are able to recognise these words, as it will save time with the dictionary in the exam:

◆ numbers, including times, dates, temperatures, distances and prices

◆ days, months, weeks and years

◆ jobs and professions

◆ school, including subjects studied

◆ food and drink

◆ family members

◆ the weather

◆ hobbies and sports

◆ daily routine and household tasks

◆ places in town

◆ methods of transport

◆ houses and rooms in the house

◆ question words and phrases

READING: FOUNDATION AND GENERAL LEVELS

1 You read this article in a French newspaper.

Pas d'alcool pour les mineurs dans les parcs

Le maire de Cholet vient d'interdire la consommation d'alcool aux mineurs dans les espaces verts, entre 20h et 6h du matin. Il veut empêcher les jeunes de se regrouper pour boire. La police pourra ramener les contrevenants chez eux.

The article explains rules about young people and alcohol.

(a) Where and when should they not drink? **3**

....

....

(b) What might happen if they are caught? **1**

....

2 You read this article about how to deal with hedgehogs in your garden.

C'est l'automne, et je vois un jeune hérisson dans mon jardin. Qu'est-ce que je dois faire?

Avant l'hiver, le hérisson cherche à économiser autant de calories que possible. Quand il fait trop froid et la nourriture devient trop difficile à trouver, il entre en hibernation dans un nid bien isolé. Mais pendant tout

continued ➤

l'automne, il mange comme quatre pour accumuler un maximum de réserves de graisse.

Ainsi, un jeune hérisson, pour avoir de bonnes chances de survivre, doit atteindre un poids de 450g avant de commencer son hibernation.

Si tu trouves un jeune hérisson encore actif à l'automne, tu peux donc lui offrir de la nourriture et un bon nid bien isolé.

(a) What **two** reasons are given for hedgehogs going into hibernation?   **2**

....

....

(b) What **two** pieces of advice are you given if you find a hedgehog?   **2**

....

....

3 You read the rest of the article: it gives you advice on what kinds of food you should give a hedgehog.

Quels aliments?

Le mieux est de mettre, dans une assiette ou un bol:

❑ de la nourriture pour chaton (ou pour chat);

❑ comme pour un chat, des restes de table (mais pas trop salés);

❑ des petits yaourts: les offrir au hérisson dans leur petit pot de plastique, en enlevant simplement le carré de papier alu qui les ferme – cela empêche les chats de les manger, mais permet aux jeunes hérissons de manger le petit yaourt, avec leur *museau pointu.

*museau – *muzzle*

Are the following statements **true** or **false**? Write T or F in the boxes below.

You should put out food on a plate	
You should keep the cat away	
You should never put out leftover food	
Put out yoghurts in their pots	

4 You read this article about the environment in a French magazine.

Des chiffres-clés sur la planète

Une personne sur cinq vit avec moins d'un dollar par jour
25% de la population mondiale vit sans électricité
Les glaciers de l'Himalaya pourraient disparaître d'ici à 2035
815 millions de personnes sont sous-alimentées
15% de la population mondiale possède 80% des richesses
20% de la population mondiale n'a pas accès à l'eau potable
Toutes les deux secondes, une forêt de la taille d'un terrain de football disparaît

Complete the following sentences.   5

(a) One person in 5 lives on...

(b) 25% of the world's population lives...

(c) 20% of the world doesn't have...

(d) Every two seconds ....

.... disappears

5 You read this article about a new project involving a giant boat.

Freedom

Un projet fou est prévu pour l'an 2007: une ville flottante de 1,6 km de long. Quelques 115 000 habitants pourraient y entrer. Ce supergrand bateau, *Freedom*, va faire le tour de la terre tous les 2 ans. Sur le *Freedom*, les gens vivent et travaillent dans des restaurants, des magasins et des bureaux. Il y a aussi des écoles, des bibliothèques, un hôpital, des banques, etc.

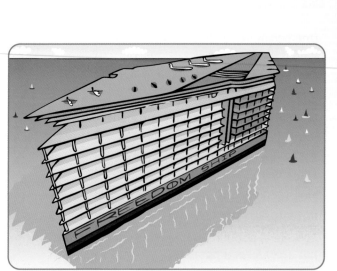

Pour les heures de loisir, le *Freedom* va avoir aussi des parcs, des terrains de tennis, et même des pistes cyclables. Des toilettes spéciales avec incinérateur électrique détruisent les déchets plutôt que les jeter dans la mer.

(a) How big is the boat? Mention **two** things.　　　　　　　　**2**

....

....

(b) What leisure facilities will there be? Mention **two** things.　　**2**

....

....

6 In this article, a French musician tells how she worked to help fund her studies.

Musicienne

J'avais treize ans lorsque des circonstances familiales ont précipité mon entrée dans le monde du travail. En plus de poursuivre des études de musique au conservatoire, j'avais deux emplois. Comme ma spécialité était le piano, j'ai accepté un petit contrat d'accompagnatrice pour un professeur de ballet. Je jouais aux classes de danse le vendredi et le samedi, et, en semaine, après mes cours de musique, j'aidais mon père dans son magasin de chaussures. J'ai dû acquérir une discipline de travail. Ma mère m'y a beaucoup aidée. Elle m'a montré comment structurer mon temps, organiser mes activités.

Complete the following sentences. **6**

(a) She started work when she was…………………………………… years old.

(b) As well as her studies, she had…………………………….…..……………..

(c) She played piano on………………………………………….……………….

(d) During the week, after school she …………………………....……………
………………………………..in……………………………......……………..

READING: CREDIT LEVEL

1 You read this advice for young French people considering a career as a hair stylist.

Coiffeur

Il n'est pas simple de trouver une place dans le monde de la coiffure aujourd'hui.

De nombreux apprentis ne trouvent pas d'emploi après l'obtention de leur diplôme. Et le secteur est marqué par de toutes petites structures: leur taille moyenne est de 2,9 personnes par salon. La profession est encore très dominée par les femmes: seuls 15% des coiffeurs sont des hommes. Mais les employeurs assurent qu'un bon coiffeur jeune va trouver un emploi, s'il est doué ...

(a) Why do young people find it hard to get a job as a hair stylist when they have finished their training? **1**

....

(b) What advice is given to young men wanting to enter the profession? **2**

....

....

Que fait-il? La majorité des coiffeurs travaillent en salon de coiffure. Le rôle de ce salarié consiste à accueillir les clients, les écouter et les conseiller sur la coupe choisie. Il procède alors au shampooing, à la coupe et éventuellement à d'autres soins: couleur, permanente, etc.

(c) What would a hair stylist be expected to do before shampooing?
Mention **three** things.   **3**

....

....

....

Comment est le travail? Le métier de coiffeur implique de longs moments en position debout, dans des postures fatigantes pour les bras, le dos et les jambes. Il est déconseillé aux jeunes qui ont des allergies de se lancer dans le secteur car l'utilisation de produits parfois toxiques et les ambiances humides et chaudes pourraient être très problematiques. Les horaires sont assez irréguliers et normalement on travaille le samedi.

(d) What disadvantages are mentioned to the job? Mention any **four** things.   **4**

....

....

....

....

2 You read this article about the health of French people.

Exercice!

Imaginez une pilule miracle ... une pilule énergisante, qui aiderait à contrôler des problèmes de santé comme les maladies cardiaques, le diabète, l'obésité, certains types de cancer, la dépression, l'arthrite, etc.

(a) What could this miracle pill do?   **1**

....

Eh bien, bonne nouvelle: cette pilule miracle existe. Son nom: l'exercice! De source naturelle (ne contient aucun agent chimique ni additif), elle doit être consommée une fois par jour à l'heure de votre choix et il est préférable de la savourer pendant au moins trente minutes pour retirer le maximum de profits; elle se présente sous différentes formes (marche, patinage, natation, ski, jogging, bicyclette); elle peut se prendre autant à l'intérieur qu'à l'extérieur; et elle peut même parfois remplacer d'autres pilules!

(b) How often and when should the miracle medicine be taken? **2**

....

....

(c) What special advantage does the pill have? **1**

....

Les faits sont là. Pourtant, nous sommes confrontés à une évidence: l'activité physique régulière apporte des effets bénéfiques sur la santé mais plus de la moitié des Français sont inactifs ou ne sont pas suffisamment actifs pour en retirer ces bienfaits.

(d) Why is there a problem for French people? Mention **two** things. **2**

....

....

3 You read this article about how young people in France are addicted to their mobile phones.

Les accros du portable

Dans le vestibule chez la famille Martin, on peut apercevoir, dans un coin, un tas de chaussures, mais aussi une rangée de téléphones portables. Tous les soirs rentrés chez eux, Vanessa, 14 ans, Raphaël, 16 ans, Marie, 44 ans, et Patrick, 45 ans, branchent les petites boîtes colorées pour les recharger. C'est devenu un rituel en vigueur dans de nombreuses familles en France. Raphaël: "Depuis que j'en ai un, j'ai acquis de nombreuses libertés: je peux aller seul en ville, j'ai la permission de minuit dans les soirées."

(a) What can you see in the hall as you come in? Mention **two** things.　　　**2**

....

....

(b) What advantages has a phone brought Raphaël? Mention **two** things.　　**2**

....

....

La mère de Raphaël et de Vanessa exprime sa satisfaction: depuis que ses enfants possèdent un portable, "ça a libéré ma ligne" déclare-t-elle. Elle se sent sécurisée de savoir qu'ils peuvent appeler en cas d'urgence. Enfin, elle apprécie de ne plus avoir à bagarrer pour les factures de téléphone. Désormais, carte ou forfait, ses enfants gèrent leurs dépenses avec leur argent de poche. Mais au début, l'usage du mobile n'était pas si simple: "Ce n'est pas toujours fiable", "on n'entend pas bien" et, "c'est cher" disaient les enfants.

(c) What **three** advantages does Mme Martin find with the mobiles?　　**3**

....

....

....

(d) Mention any **two** disadvantages the children found with the mobiles.　　**2**

....

....

Mais, après quelque temps, ils trouvent ça génial. On peut appeler de n'importe quel endroit, décider à la dernière minute ce qu'on va faire le soir, et téléphoner à n'importe quelle heure (si le portable est branché, cela signifie qu'on ne dérange pas); être appelé même la nuit, sans réveiller les parents; enfin, être sûr que ses messages ne seront pas écoutés, parce qu'ils ne sont plus sur le téléphone familial.

(e) Give **three** reasons they are now happy with their phones.　　**3**

....

....

....

4 You read this article about a woman who got on in the world.

Adrienne Clarkson, gouverneure générale du Canada

J'ai débarqué au Canada avec ma famille en 1942. J'avais trois ans. Avec d'autres réfugiés de Hong Kong, nous avions voyagé à bord d'un bateau de la Croix-Rouge. Je me souviens encore des bombes japonaises qui pleuvaient sur la ville. Nous avions peu d'argent, et notre nouvelle vie à Ottawa n'a jamais été facile. Mon père me répétait qu'il fallait travailler pour obtenir quelque chose sur cette terre. Dès que j'ai été en âge de travailler, mes parents m'ont encouragée à prendre un petit emploi.

(a) Why was her early life difficult? Mention **three** things.   **3**

....

....

....

En 1958, A.J. Frieman était "le" grand magasin d'Ottawa. À 17 ans, mon secondaire terminé, j'y ai décroché un emploi dans le bureau. Comme personne ne savait exactement en quoi consistait ma fonction, j'ai décidé d'en faire le plus possible. Je répondais au téléphone, j'écoutais les réclamations des clients et j'apprenais à tester les tubes de leur télévision. Personne ne m'avait imposé ces besognes. Je savais seulement que, si j'assumais de plus en plus de responsabilités, je finirais par me rendre indispensable à mes employeurs.

(b) What tasks did she decide to take on in her work? Mention **two** things.   **2**

....

....

(c) Why did she decide to take these on?   **2**

....

....

Huit ans plus tard, quand j'ai commencé à travailler à la télévision, je n'ai jamais refusé une tâche, si humble soit-elle. De tous les gens avec qui j'ai collaboré à la télévision, ceux dont je garde le meilleur souvenir sont ceux qui étaient capables de mettre l'épaule à la roue quand c'était nécessaire. Aujourd'hui, lorsque je vois quelqu'un prendre des initiatives, je souris en me disant: "En voilà un qui connaît le secret du travail: si tu veux faire ton chemin en ce monde, rends-toi indispensable."

(d) Who does she remember best from her days in television?   **2**

....

....

(e) What does she think is the secret of getting on at work?   **2**

....

....

ANSWERS TO THE READING TESTS

Foundation and General levels

1 Pas d'alcool pour les mineurs dans les parcs

(a) They should not drink in **parks/green spaces** between **10 at night** and **6 in the morning** (Make sure you know your times!)

(b) They will be **taken home** (*Chez* is the important word here!)

2 C'est l'automne, et je vois un jeune hérisson dans mon jardin.

(a) it is **cold**, it is **hard to find food**

(b) **feed it, give it a nest**

3 Quels aliments?

You should put out food on a plate	T
You should keep the cat away	F
You should never put out leftover food	F
Put out yoghurts in their pots	T

4 Des chiffres-clés sur la planète

(a) One person in 5 lives on **less than a dollar a day**

(b) 25% of the world's population lives **without electricity**

(c) 20% of the world doesn't have **(access to) drinking water**

(d) Every two seconds, **a forest the size of a football pitch** disappears (2 marks)

5 Freedom

(a) **1.6 kilometres long, can hold 115,000 people**

(b) **parks, tennis courts, cycle paths** (any two)

6 Musicienne

(a) She started work when she was **thirteen** years old

(b) As well as her studies, she had **two jobs**

(c) She played piano on **Friday and Saturday**

(d) During the week, after school she **helped her father in his (shoe) shop**

Credit level

1 **Coiffeur**

   (a) **Most shops are very small (they only have an average of 2.9 people)**

   (b) **Most hair stylists are women, but a good male hair stylist will get a job**

   (c) **welcome the customers, listen to them, advise them** (three verbs!)

   (d) **a long time standing, in tiring positions, not a good idea if you have allergies, hot humid atmosphere not great, irregular hours, have to work on Saturdays** (any four)

2 **Exercice!**

   (a) **give you energy, or help health problems**

   (b) **once a day, for at least 30 minutes**

   (c) **it contains no chemicals,** or **you can take it in a variety of ways,** or **you can take it indoors or outdoors**

   (d) **although exercise has health benefits, half of the French are inactive or do not do enough exercise to get the benefits**

3 **Les accros du portable**

   (a) **shoes**, and a *row* of **mobile phones**

   (b) **he has more freedom, he can go into town alone, he can stay out until midnight** (any two)

   (c) **it has freed up her phone line, she feels safer knowing they can call in an emergency, she doesn't have fights about the phone bill any more**

   (d) **you couldn't always rely on it, you couldn't hear well, it was dear, it came from their pocket money** (any two)

   (e) **you can phone from anywhere, decide at the last moment what you are doing, phone at any time, be called at night, know that no one can hear your call** (any three)

4 **Adrienne Clarkson, gouverneure générale du Canada**

   (a) **she was a refugee, she was bombed by the Japanese, they had little money**

   (b) **she answered the phone, listened to customer complaints, tested television tubes** (any two)

   (c) **if she took on responsibilities, her employers would find she was indispensable**

   (d) **people who could work hard (put their shoulder to the wheel), when it was needed**

   (e) **if you want to get on, make yourself indispensable**

Chapter 6

LISTENING

Introduction

Listening is worth **one-sixth** of your overall Standard Grade result: it will be tested in an external exam, and the test at each level will last about 20 to 25 minutes. You will not be able to use a dictionary for this exam, so you need to be prepared for the exam in advance, and make sure you know the basic vocabulary which comes up again and again.

To help with your revision, the Listening passages in this book are separated into topic areas: in the real exam, there will be a variety of topic areas covered within each paper.

The key to this exam is concentration, as the passages come at set intervals, and you cannot ask to hear them again if you were not paying attention! The French on which your questions will be based is repeated three times, with a gap of a few seconds between each passage. For Foundation and General levels, there is always a 30-second gap between each separate passage, and at Credit level this gap is usually 40 seconds. Each question from the listening tests in this book has been recorded as a separate track on the accompanying CD, to help you find the parts you want to practise easily. The track numbers are given after the questions (*in brackets*). The marks available are given in **bold**. If you get your question answered very quickly, then it is easy to lose concentration while waiting for the next passage: try to prepare for the next question by reading it in advance, so that when you hear the French, you are focused and know what you are listening out for.

Try not to write anything down during the first listening, even if you know the answer: you will have plenty of time later. It is very tempting to dash things down, so that you don't forget them, but realistically that is not going to happen! You also risk missing out important details, because you are concentrating on writing. Use that first listening to make sure you hear everything, and to give you a guide for which bit you have to listen to extra carefully for details you are required to give in your answer.

Make sure you know what you are listening for: particularly at the end of the General paper and in the Credit paper there will be lots of information you don't need, which just acts as interference when you are listening. Focus on what is needed for the answer.

If you are not sure of an answer, go ahead and guess, as what you guess will be a secret between the examiner and you! Try however to make it an intelligent guess:

if what you have written looks daft to you, then it probably is: your answer should make sense.

If the answer asks for two things, just give two things! The examiner will only give you marks for the first two things you write down, and you will get no credit for something correct that is written later on in the answer, if there is a wrong answer given before it.

Vocabulary tips

There are some vocabulary areas which always come up in the Listening exam, and it is important that you know and are able to recognise these words, as you do not have a dictionary in the exam. These areas are listed below:

◆ numbers, including times, dates, temperatures, distances and prices

◆ days, months, weeks and years

◆ jobs and professions

◆ school, including subjects studied

◆ food and drink

◆ family members

◆ the weather

◆ hobbies and sports

◆ daily routine and household tasks

◆ places in town

◆ methods of transport

◆ houses and rooms in the house

◆ question words and phrases

LISTENING: FOUNDATION AND GENERAL LEVELS

1 Questions about school

You will hear Thierry talking about school: before you listen, revise the days of the week, school subjects and times. Anything else you have learned on this topic is also worth looking over.

1   At what time does Thierry's school day start and finish? When does he have a break, and for how long?   (2)   **4**

start	
finish	
break starts	
length of break	

2   Which days does he go to school? Tick each day he is at school. Which is his favourite day? Mark it with a tick.   (3)   **6**

	school?	favourite
Monday		
Tuesday		
Wednesday		
Thursday		
Friday		
Saturday		

3   At what time does he have to get up for school? How does he get to school?   (4)   **2**

He gets up at.. and goes to school on.................

4   How long has he been at his present school?   (5)   **1**

He has been there for..

5   When do classes start in the afternoon?   (6)   **1**

Classes start at ....

6   Why does he mention Madame Albert? Mention **two** things.   (7)   **2**

....

....

7   What does he think of her? Mention **two** things.   (8)   **2**

....

....

8   What classes does he have on a Thursday morning? What does he think
of them?   (9)   **4**

subject	opinion

9   What does he do on Wednesday lunchtimes? Mention **two** things.
Why does he do this?   (10)   **3**

He   ....

....

This is because   ....

10 Why is he looking forward to this Friday? Mention **two** things.   (11)   **2**

....

2 Questions about family and daily routine

You will hear Alain talking about his family: before you listen, revise the vocabulary
for daily routine and family members. You should also look at the vocabulary for
household tasks, as well as words to describe people.

1   Who does Alain live with? Which ages does he mention?   (12)   **5**

person	age

2   Which members of his family does he mention? Mention one thing he says
about each one.   (13)   **3**

family member	comment
1	
2	
3	

3   He describes his brother. Which of these people is his brother?   *(14)*

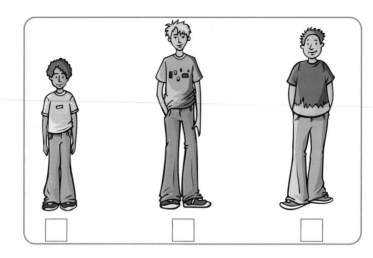

☐   ☐   ☐

4   How does his morning routine work?   *(15)*   **3**

	activity
6.15	
7.00	
7.30	

5   Who are they going to visit tomorrow?   *(16)*   **1**

    ....

6   What will they do there?   *(17)*   **1**

    ....

7   Who is coming to visit next week? What does he think of her? Why?   *(18)*   **3**

    His .... is going to visit next week.

    He thinks ....

    because ....

8   What does he have to do to help at home? Tick the correct activities.   (19)   **3**

9   He mentions two things he does to earn extra pocket money. What are these activities? What does he think of these activities?   (20)   **4**

activities	opinion

10 You meet his sister: what two questions does she ask you?   (21)   **2**

	asked
How long are you here for?	
How did you get here?	
Have you been to France before?	
What do you think of France?	

3 Questions about home, food and drink

You will hear Brigitte talking about her home. Before you listen, revise the vocabulary for these topic areas. You should also look at the vocabulary for eating, drinking and shopping.

1 Which of these houses does Brigitte live in? *(22)* **1**

2 Which rooms does she mention in the house? Tick the box if she mentions the room. *(23)* **4**

kitchen		living room	
bathroom		dining room	
bedroom		cellar	
utility room		attic	

3 What three things does she tell you about her house? *(24)* **3**

Her house does not have ……………………………………………………………

It does have a ……………………………………………………………………

Her house is very ……………………………………………………………………

4   Brigitte tells you about where her older sister, Marie (a student), now lives: what information does she give you? Tick the correct boxes.   *(25)*   **4**

Her sister lives:

on the first floor	
on the ground floor	
in a flat with one bedroom	
alone	
with another student	
in a place with a balcony	
in a place with a shower	

5   You are about to have lunch: what will you be having to eat? Choose the correct illustration.   *(26)*   **1**

6   Her mother asks you to go to the supermarket for her: what does she ask you to get?   *(27)*   **4**

a kilo of	
a tin of	
250 grammes of	
a bottle of	

7   While you are at the supermarket, you decide to buy some chocolates to take home as a present: how much do they cost?   *(28)*   **1**

....

8 On the way home you meet Brigitte. She has a message to get something as well: what must she buy? Where will she get this?   *(29)*   **2**

She is going to buy.............................. at the ....

9 You are in the restaurant with your penfriend's parents. The waiter offers you a choice of starters: what choices are you offered? Tick three boxes.   *(30)*   **3**

tomato soup	
tomato salad	
snails	
ham	
green salad	

10 Brigitte's father offers you a drink with your meal: what choices are you offered?   *(31)*   **3**

1	
2	
3	

4 Questions about work and hobbies

You will hear Sandrine talking about her free time and work: before you listen, revise the vocabulary for these topic areas. You should also look at the vocabulary relating to jobs and professions.

1 Which of these hobbies does Sandrine mention?   *(32)*   **3**

going to cinema		going out with friends	
cycling		horse riding	
swimming		reading	

2 What does she think of television? Why does she think this?   *(33)*   **2**

She finds TV......................................, because.........................

3   On Wednesday afternoon Sandrine is in two sport clubs: which ones does she mention? Tick two boxes.   (*34*)   **2**

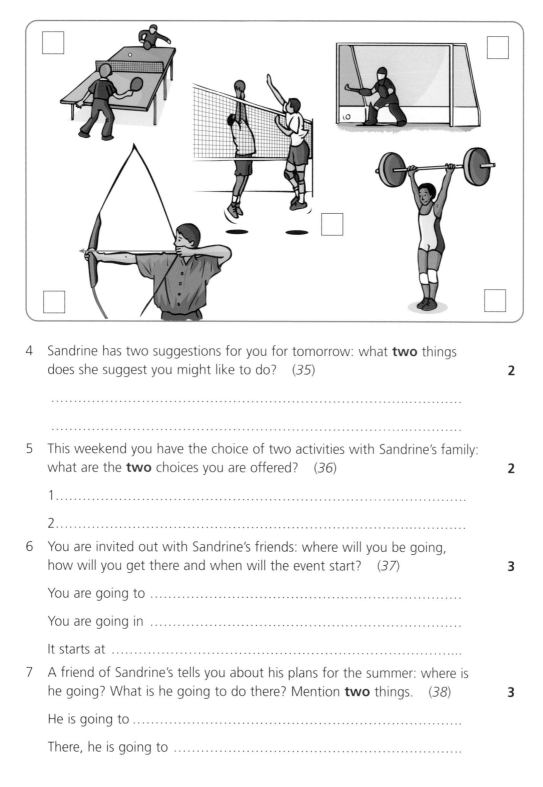

4   Sandrine has two suggestions for you for tomorrow: what **two** things does she suggest you might like to do?   (*35*)   **2**

....

....

5   This weekend you have the choice of two activities with Sandrine's family: what are the **two** choices you are offered?   (*36*)   **2**

1...

2...

6   You are invited out with Sandrine's friends: where will you be going, how will you get there and when will the event start?   (*37*)   **3**

You are going to ....

You are going in ....

It starts at ....

7   A friend of Sandrine's tells you about his plans for the summer: where is he going? What is he going to do there? Mention **two** things.   (*38*)   **3**

He is going to ....

There, he is going to ....

8   Sandrine tells you about her part-time job: when does she work?
    How much does she earn?   *(39)*   **6**

days	and
times	until
earnings	per

9   Sandrine's mother tells you about her job. Complete the sentences.   *(40)*   **3**

Her mother works as a……………………………………….. She has worked

there for…………………… She works in…………………………………………

10 She tells you about her brother and sisters: what jobs do they do?
    Match the names to the jobs by drawing connecting arrows.   *(41)*

Léon	nurse
	taxi driver
	shop assistant
Nathalie	lorry driver
	cook
Virginie	farmer

11 Sandrine's mother tells you more about her job: what does she like and dislike
    about it?   *(42)*

    ………………………………………………………………………………………………………

5 Questions about transport and around town

You will hear Nathalie talking about places in town. Before you listen, revise the vocabulary for these topic areas. You should also look at the vocabulary for the weather.

1   Your penfriend, Nathalie, mentions how you are getting to school the next day. Which methods of transport will you use? Tick three boxes.   (*43*)   **3**

2   Where exactly is her school?   (*44*)   **2**

Her school is in the………………………, next to the………………..……

3   At what time does the bus leave to get you home? How much will it cost?   (*45*)

The bus leaves at………………………… Your ticket will cost……………

4   This Saturday your penfriend proposes an excursion: where to? How does she propose you get there? What would decide which method of transport you would use?   (*46*)   **5**

You are going to ………………………………………..

You'll go by………………………………if………………………………

You'll go by………………………………if………………………………

5   She tells you about the holiday she went on last year: how did she get there? What was the weather like?   (*47*)   **3**

She went by …………………………… and …………………………………

The weather was …………………………, but ……………………………

6   The school is organising a trip for you the next day: where are you going? How will you get there?   *(48)*   **2**

The trip is to…………………………… You are going there by…………

7   Your penfriend's mother suggests somewhere to go when you get back from school. Where does she suggest? How do you get there?   *(49)*   **4**

She suggests you go to…………………………… It is in the centre of town, near ……………………… From the bus stop, you take the ………………… street on the …………………………

8   You are looking for postcards to send home: where does Nathalie suggest you look? Mention **two** places.   *(50)*   **2**

………………………………………………………………………………

………………………………………………………………………………

9   You are going to visit Nathalie's grandparents: where do they live?   *(51)*   **3**

They live ……………………………… away, to the …………………………

They live in a…………………………………………………

10 What does Nathalie think of where they live? Mention **one** advantage, and **one** disadvantage.   *(52)*   **2**

………………………………………………………………………………

………………………………………………………………………………

LISTENING: CREDIT LEVEL

At this level, the texts you hear will be longer, and there will be fewer guidelines on answering the questions. You should not assume that the person speaking will be a penfriend.

1 Talking about future plans

You will hear a series of questions related to a young person's plans for the future.

1 Vincent is about to leave school and go to university: how has he found school? Mention **three** things.   (53)   **3**

....

....

....

2 a) Where is he going to study? b) Mention **any two** things about the place.   (54)   **3**

....

....

....

3 Where will he stay while he is there? Give **four** details.   (55)   **4**

....

....

....

4 What plans does he have for this summer? Mention any **four** things.   (56)   **4**

....

....

....

5 What does he say about marriage? Mention **three** details.   (57)   **3**

....

....

....

6 How will he support himself at university? Mention **three** things.   (58)   **3**

....

....

....

2 Talking about a visit

You will hear a series of questions related to a French woman's trip to another country.

1 Lucie went to South America: why did she go there? Mention **three** things. (59)   **3**

....

....

....

2 Where exactly did she go? Mention **three** things.   (60)   **3**

....

....

....

3 Where did she stay while she was there? Give **four** details.   (61)   **4**

....

....

....

4 What problems did she have there? Mention any **four** things.   (62)   **4**

....

....

....

5 What does she say she liked most? Mention **three** details.   (63)   **3**

....

....

....

6 How will she feel now she is back home? Mention **three** things.   (64)   **3**

....

....

....

3 Interview with a young film star

You will hear a series of questions related to a young person's career on TV and in the cinema.

1 Louis is a teenage film star. How did this happen? Mention **three** things.   (65) **3**

....

....

....

2 Where is he going to film next? Mention **three** things.   (66)   **3**

....

....

....

3 Where will he stay while he is there? Give **four** details.   (67)   **4**

....

....

....

4 What plans does he have for the future? Mention any **four** things.   (68)   **4**

....

....

....

5 What does he say about his TV series? Mention **three** details.   (69)   **3**

....

....

....

6 How do his parents support him? Mention **three** things.   (70)   **3**

....

....

....

TRANSCRIPTS AND ANSWERS TO THE LISTENING TESTS

Transcripts: Foundation and General levels

1 Questions about school

1 Au collège, les cours commencent le matin à huit heures et demie, et terminent à cinq heures de l'après-midi. Le matin à dix heures et demie, on a une récré de quinze minutes.

2 On a école du lundi jusqu'au vendredi. Mon jour favori, c'est le mercredi, car l'école finit à midi et demi.

3 Le matin, je me lève à six heures et quart pour me préparer. Je vais au collège à pied, car c'est à 500 mètres de chez nous.

4 Je suis au Collège Desmoulins depuis trois ans, et je suis en quatrième maintenant.

5 L'après-midi, les cours commencent à deux heures.

6 Ma prof d'anglais, elle s'appelle Mme Albert: elle nous donne beaucoup de devoirs.

7 Je la trouve assez sévère, mais elle nous aide quand nous avons des problèmes.

8 Le jeudi matin, j'ai une heure du géo, que je trouve très dur, puis informatique et je trouve ça passionnant!

9 Les mercredis on ne mange pas à la cantine: je vais dans le centre-ville avec mes copains, car l'après-midi il n'y a pas de cours.

10 J'attends ce vendredi avec impatience: c'est le dernier jour avant les vacances. Après, nous avons les vacances de Pâques.

2 Questions about family and daily routine

1 Chez nous il y a ma mère, mon frère Nico qui a 13 ans, et ma sœur aînée Nadine, qui a 19 ans.

2 Mon père habite maintenant en Belgique. Mon frère Nico, je le trouve très, très agaçant. Ma sœur Nadine est très gentille. Tu vas bien l'aimer.

3 Mon frère Nico est assez petit, il a les cheveux bruns et bouclés.

4 Le matin, je me lève à six heures et quart. Je vais me laver dans la salle de bains à sept heures. À 7h30, je prends mon petit déjeuner.

5 Demain, on va rendre visite à mes grands-parents.

6 Là, on va fêter l'anniversaire de mon grand-père, qui va avoir 70 ans.

TRANSCRIPTS AND ANSWERS TO THE LISTENING TESTS

7 Ma tante Hélène va venir chez nous mercredi prochain. Je la trouve très intéressante, car elle travaille a la télé à Paris.

8 Pour aider à la maison, il faut que je passe l'aspirateur, que je mette la table, et aussi que je range la vaisselle dans le lave-vaisselle.

9 En plus, pour gagner de l'argent, je lave la voiture de ma mère, une activité que je déteste, et je l'aide a faire le jardin. Ça, c'est bien.

10 Salut! Combien de temps est-ce que tu vas passer ici? Qu'est-ce que tu penses de notre pays?

3 Questions about home, food and drink

1 J'habite une maison en plein centre-ville.

2 Chez nous, il y a une cuisine, trois chambres, un grand séjour et, bien sûr, une salle de bains!

3 On n'a pas de garage, mais il y a un petit jardin, et la maison est très jolie.

4 Ma sœur Marie, qui est étudiante, habite maintenant dans un petit appartement avec une seule chambre, à Lille: c'est au premier étage, c'est parfait pour une personne, et il y a une douche.

5 Aujourd'hui on mange du poulet et du riz pour le déjeuner, et après, des fruits.

6 Tu peux aller au supermarché pour moi, et acheter un kilo de pommes de terre, une boîte de haricots, 250 grammes de beurre, et une bouteille d'eau?

7 Les pralinés, ça coûte €13.50.

8 Ah bonjour! Tu m'accompagnes au magasin de sport? Je dois acheter de nouvelles baskets.

9 Alors pour commencer, on propose une salade verte, une potage de tomates, ou du jambon.

10 Qu'est-ce que tu veux boire? Tu préfères du coca, du jus d'orange, ou un verre de vin?

4 Questions about work and hobbies

1 Dans mon temps libre, j'aime bien sortir avec mes copines, faire du vélo, et faire de la natation.

2 Je trouve la télé ennuyeuse, il y a trop de sport à la télé.

3 Mais j'aime faire du sport. Le mercredi je joue au volley et au tennis de table.

4 Demain, si tu veux, on peut aller faire les magasins l'après-midi, puis le soir on pourrait aller au cinéma.

5 Ce week-end on peut aller aux montagne pour faire une promenade, ou on peut aller au bord de la mer pour faire de la voile avec mon oncle. Qu'est-ce que tu préfères?

6 Ce soir on est invité au restaurant pour fêter l'anniversaire de mon copain Thomas. Maman va nous emmener en voiture, et on doit être au restaurant pour 7h30.

7 Cet été, je vais aller aux États-Unis. Je vais habiter chez mon correspondant Bob, et on va faire la descente d'une rivière en canoë.

8 Normalement je travaille dans une boulangerie le samedi et le dimanche, de sept heures jusqu'à dix heures du matin. Je gagne 20 euros par jour.

9 Je travaille depuis douze ans comme secrétaire: je travaille dans le bureau du lycée.

10 Mon frère Léon travaille à Bruxelles comme chauffeur de camion, ma sœur Nathalie est infirmière, et ma petite sœur Virginie est vendeuse chez Monoprix.

11 Ce que j'aime dans mon travail, c'est que j'ai de longues vacances, car on ne travaille que quand l'école est ouverte. Mais ce n'est pas très bien payé.

5 Questions about transport and round about town

1 Demain, maman nous emmène en voiture à l'arrêt d'autobus, on passe dix minutes dans l'autobus, et puis il faut cinq minutes à pied pour arriver au collège.

2 L'école est en centre-ville, à côté de la mairie.

3 On rentre à cinq heures et quart: tu dois payer €2 pour le trajet.

4 Ce samedi je propose d'aller au Château de Fougères. S'il fait beau, nous irons à vélo, mais s'il pleut, papa nous emmènera en voiture.

5 L'année dernière nous sommes allés en Corse: dix heures en voiture jusqu'à Marseille, et puis trois heures en bateau. Il faisait très beau, mais il y avait du vent! J'avais quand même peur.

6 Demain on a organisé un voyage dans une ville très pittoresque, Dinan, près de la mer: on y va par le train de Rennes!

7 Cet après-midi, si tu veux, tu peux aller à la maison des jeunes. C'est en centre-ville, à côté de la piscine. Lorsque tu descends de l'autobus, tu prends la première rue à gauche, et la voilà!

8 Pour les cartes postales, ou tu peux aller au syndicat d'initiative ou bien aux Galeries Lafayette, le grand magasin.

9 Ce soir on va rendre visite à mes grands-parents, qui habitent à trente kilomètres d'ici, au nord-ouest. Ils habitent un tout petit village.

10 C'est très joli là où ils habitent, mais c'est aussi très tranquille. Je n'aimerais pas vivre là-bas.

Transcipts: Credit level

1 Talking about future plans

1 Je n'ai pas aimé l'école, parce que les journées étaient très longues, surtout parce que j'avais un trajet de quarante minutes en car chaque jour, et deux heures des devoirs chaque soir.

2 Je vais aller en fac, à Nice: je veux assister à des cours de langues vivantes, et l'université de Nice est connue pour l'anglais et l'italien. En plus, la ville de Nice offre beaucoup d'activités culturelles!

3 Je vais loger chez mon copain Éric, qui est à Nice depuis un an déjà. Il a un appartement dans un immeuble en centre-ville. C'est cher, mais il m'est important de vivre en centre-ville.

4 Cet été je vais travailler chez mon oncle pour gagner de l'argent pour l'université. Il tient une ferme dans le sud-ouest de la France, et je vais faire les vendange. Je travaillerai pendant six semaines.

5 Je pense me marier un jour, mais seulement dans dix ans, lorsque j'aurai terminé mes études. Je ne voudrais pas être marié et étudiant en même temps.

6 Quand je serai à Nice, je sais que je devrai trouver un petit boulot pour pouvoir payer le loyer de mon appartement. J'ai déjà travaillé comme serveur, et je vais chercher du travail dans un restaurant.

2 Talking about a visit

1 Je suis allée en Amérique du Sud, car mon père est espagnol, et je parle la langue, et aussi car je voulais faire un très long voyage. C'était un voyage qui m'emmenait loin de chez moi.

2 Je suis allée en Patagonie, au sud de l'Argentine: ce n'était pas très loin de l'océan Antarctique.

3 J'ai passé le premier mois dans une famille argentine, dans leur ferme. Après, j'ai voyagé dans le vrai sud, et j'ai dormi dans une tente la plupart du temps: quelquefois je me suis installée dans une pension pour une nuit.

4 Je supportais très mal la température: il faisait très froid, et il y avait toujours un vent très fort. Un jour le vent a pris ma tente, et toutes mes affaires ont été mouillées par la pluie.

5 Ce qui m'a impressionnée le plus, c'était la solitude, et le fait que tout le monde était beaucoup moins stressé que chez nous. Tout le monde prend son temps. La vie est plus lente.

6 J'ai changé depuis mon voyage. Je trouve l'environnement beaucoup plus important, et je vais chercher un emploi qui me permettra de sauvegarder la nature, en France.

3 Interview with a young film star

1 Tout a commencé quand j'avais treize ans: j'ai participé à un concours qui cherchait un acteur pour une publicité: j'ai gagné, et la publicité a été un grand succès.

2 Au mois de novembre, je vais apparaître dans un film qui traite d'une famille qui se perd dans la montagne: ce film aura lieu dans les Alpes, près du mont Blanc, et aussi en Suisse.

3 On logera dans un petit hôtel près de Grenoble, mais, lorsqu'on tourne a le film, on logera aussi dans un refuge en montagne, très haut en altitude, et à 15 kilomètres du prochain village.

4 Après cela, je vais arrêter de filmer pendant un an, pour pouvoir me concentrer sur mes études pour mon baccalauréat. Je vais habiter à Paris, chez mes grands-parents. Puis j'aimerais aller en fac, peut-être aux États-Unis.

5 La série qui traitait d'un élève au collège, que j'ai tournée pour la télé, je l'ai fini maintenant. Je suis trop âgé pour ce rôle, et on cherche un remplacent.

6 J'ai pu faire tout ce travail parce que mes parents m'ont beaucoup d'aidé. Ma mère a quitté son travail pour pouvoir s'occuper de moi, et mon père, qui est professeur, m'a aidé à faire mes devoirs, quand j'avais des problèmes.

Answers: Foundation and General levels

1 Questions about school

1

start	8.30
finish	5.00
break starts	10.30
length of break	15 minutes

2

	school?	favourite
Monday	✓	
Tuesday	✓	
Wednesday	✓	✓
Thursday	✓	
Friday	✓	
Saturday		

3   He gets up at **6.15** and goes to school on **foot**

4   He has been there for **three** years

5   Classes start at **2 p.m**.

6   **she's his English teacher**

   she gives him lots of homework

7   **she is very strict**

   she helps them with problems

8

subject	opinion
geography	hard
IT/computing	exciting/he loves it

9   He **goes into town with his friends** *or*

   he doesn't eat in the canteen

   This is because **he has no classes on Wednesday afternoon**

10 **Last day before holidays**

   Easter holiday's coming

2 Questions about family and daily routine

1

person	age
mother	
brother	13
sister	19

2

family member	comment
1 father	lives in Belgium
2 brother	annoying
3 sister	really nice/you will like her

3

4

time	activity
6.15	gets up
7.00	washes
7.30	breakfast

5 **his grandparents**

6 **it's his grandfather's birthday**

7 His **aunt** is going to visit next week. He thinks **she is interesting** because **she works in TV (in Paris)**

8

9

activities	opinion
washes car	hates that
works in garden	that is OK

10

question	asked?
How long are you here for?	✓
How did you get here?	
Have you been to France before?	
What do you think of France?	✓

3 Questions about home, food and drink

1

2

kitchen	✓	living room	✓
bathroom	✓	dining room	
bedroom	✓	cellar	
utility room		attic	

3   Her house does not have **a garage**

It does have a **garden**

Her house is very **modern**

4

on the first floor	✓
on the ground floor	
in a flat with one bedroom	✓
alone	✓
with another student	
in a place with a balcony	
in a place with a shower	✓

5   **chicken and rice, with a banana and apple on a sideplate**

6

a kilo of	**potatoes**
a tin of	**beans**
250 grammes of	**butter**
a bottle of	**water**

7   €13,50

8   She is going to buy **trainers** at the **sports shop**

9

tomato soup	✓
tomato salad	
snails	
ham	✓
green salad	✓

10

1	**coke**
2	**orange juice**
3	**wine**

4 Questions about work and hobbies

1

going to cinema		going out with friends	✓
cycling	✓	horse riding	
swimming	✓	reading	

2   She finds TV **boring**, because **there's too much sport**

HOW TO PASS STANDARD GRADE FRENCH

3

4   **shopping/shops, cinema**

5   **1 mountains for a walk**

   2 seaside to go sailing/meet uncle

6   You are going to **a restaurant**

   You are going in **(her mum's) car**

   It starts at **7.30**

7   He is going to **the USA/America**

   There, he is going to **stay with a penpal**

   go canoeing

   canoe down a river (any two)

8

days	**Saturday** and **Sunday**
times	**7** until **10**
earnings	€20 per **day**

9   Her mother works as a **secretary**. She has worked there for **12 years**.
   She works in **the school**

10

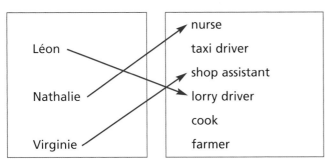

11   **Likes the (long) holidays, but it's not well paid**

5 Questions about transport and round about town

1

3

2 Her school is in the **town centre**, next to the **town hall**.

3 The bus leaves at **5.15**. Your ticket will cost **€2**.

4 You are going to **a castle (Fougères)**.

You'll go by **bike** if **the weather is nice**.

You'll go by **car** if **it's raining**.

5 She went by **car** and **boat**.

The weather was **good**, but **windy**.

6 The trip is to **Dinan/the seaside**. You are going there by **train**.

7 She suggests you go to the **youth club**. It is in the centre of town, near **the swimming pool**. From the bus stop, you take the **first** street on the **left**.

8 **tourist information** *or* **Galeries Lafayette/a department store**

9 They live **30 kilometres** away, to the **north-west**.

They live in a **village**.

10 **very pretty**

very quiet

Answers: Credit level

1 Talking about future plans

1 **didn't like it**

days were long

40 minutes on bus each day

2 hours homework per night

(any three)

2   he is going to Nice

good for languages

he can study English and Italian there

lots of cultural activities

(any two)

3   stay with Eric/his friend

who has been there a year

in a flat

it is dear

wants to stay in the centre of town

(any four)

4   work for his uncle

to earn money for university

uncle has a farm

in the south-west

work picking grapes

work for six weeks

(any four)

5   would like to get married

in ten years

when he has finished studying

would not like to be a student and married

(any three)

6   he will find a job

he has been a waiter

will look for a job in a restaurant

2 Talking about a visit

1   her father is Spanish

she speaks the language

wanted to go far way/on a long journey

2   went to Argentina

South Argentina/Patagonia

near the Antarctic

3   with a family

on their farm

in a tent

sometimes in a bed & breakfast

4   she found the temperature hard

it was cold and windy

the wind blew her tent away one day

her things got wet/were rained on

5   the solitude

the lack of stress

people aren't in a hurry

life was slow

(any three)

6   she has changed

the environment is much more important for her

she will look for a job protecting nature

3 Interview with a young film star

1   he entered a competition

to take part in an advert

he won

the advert was a great success

(any three)

2   in the Alps/the mountains

near Mont Blanc

also in Switzerland

3   in a small hotel

near Grenoble

in a mountain refuge/hut

high in the mountains

15 kilometres from the nearest village

(any four)

4   stop work for a year

concentrate on his school exams

stay with his grandparents/in Paris

go to university

maybe in the USA

(any three)

5   it was about a boy at school

he is too old for the part

they are looking for a replacement

(any three)

6   they both helped him a lot

Mum gave up work to support him

Dad is a teacher and helped him keep up with schoolwork

SPEAKING

Speaking is worth **one-third** of your overall Standard Grade result because it is such a key skill. You will have to carry out three speaking assessments over the course of the year before your exams: these assessments will be set by your teacher, and will also be marked by your teacher. They may be recorded, or they may not. This is a part of the course you can really prepare for, and do very well in, if you get the preparation right!

Your teacher will take the marks for your three tests and make an average of them: this will be your final speaking grade. If you have one poorer assessment, it's not the end of the world; the others can bring up your average.

The rules for the assessments are quite clear: there will be three different types of assessment. One will be a **prepared talk** or presentation on a subject of your choice. You will be allowed a certain number of words as notes to help you through. Your talk will be graded according to content, accuracy and a few other elements. The way of judging how well you have done is given in the grade-related Criteria your teacher will be working from: these are shown on p. 63, so that you can see what is expected of you.

The second assessment will be an informal **conversation**: this will normally involve using either *tu* or *vous*, and talking about a subject you will know in advance and can prepare. It could be the same subject you have covered for your prepared talk. There are different grade-related Criteria for this which we have also included for you (p. 67).

The third assessment will be a **role-play**, a transactional or vocational task in which you take part in a dialogue with an adult speaker of French (this may of course be your teacher), but for this task you will have to use *vous*. This will be polite, formal or vocational language. The grade-related Criteria for this are the same as those for the conversation.

You will know the topics for the more formal assessments beforehand, so you can prepare for them. This is a huge advantage!

In this chapter we will look at the three types of assessment in detail, and give you advice and support on preparing for the kind of task you are likely to be given.

The prepared talk

For this assessment, you will have to talk on a subject of your choice for up to two minutes: you can prepare this well in advance, and learn it so that you can be absolutely sure of what you have to do.

To get a General award, you will have to speak for at least a minute: you will also have to try to use a variety of tenses and structures. You should be able to give your opinion on various parts of your experience, and try to be as accurate as you can.

For Credit, you will have to speak for up to two minutes. You must be reasonably accurate in your use of French, and use tenses well. Your opinions will be more important than at General level, and you should also include reasons for some of these opinions.

Planning your talk

When you know the subject for your assessment, try to break it down into three or more sections, and prepare each one separately: this will make it easier to remember. You are allowed five headings, of eight words each, as support, so these key words should settle you into each section of your talk: this is handy, as, if you get nervous and a bit mixed up in one part, you can recover in the next part with the help of your key words.

Once you've chosen your topic area, focus on the actual language you will use. Here are a few do's and don'ts!

Do's

◆ Do look at the textbook or texts you are working from for good ideas you can use.

◆ Do make sure you understand what you are saying, or it will be very difficult to remember it properly.

◆ Do show a draft to your teacher, to get any suggestions, or so that you can make corrections.

◆ Do use a variety of structures: don't start off every sentence with *Je*, for example.

◆ Do vary your tenses, and put in some joining words like *parce que*, or *quand*.

◆ Do give your opinion, and work at having different ways of saying what you think. Look at the 'Giving opinions' section on pp. 79–80.

Don'ts

◆ Don't leave preparation to the last minute! If you start your preparation early, you'll be able to ask your teacher for advice on any vocabulary or grammar you're unsure of.

◆ Don't always stick to safe, simple language. It may be easier, but won't get the best grades. Try out some of the more impressive sentences you've learned. Note down useful vocabulary and phrases you've seen elsewhere under appropriate topic headings so you can reuse them in your speaking tests.

◆ Don't use lists of things, such as school subjects, places in town, or favourite foods to try to make your talk longer: this will count against you.

To help you prepare for a solo talk, we have selected three possible topics, and guide you through the process involved in preparing for and carrying out the assessment: you can follow the same pattern for a topic of your own choice, and you might also find Chapter 11 on writing useful to prepare for a specific speaking task.

1 *An exchange visit*
2 *Manger sain!*
3 *Mon école*

1 An exchange visit

You have been asked to present a solo talk about an exchange visit. Sort out your ideas and choose the areas that you feel most confident about: for example, your exchange partner's house or family, the school you visited or how you got there. You'll then find it easier to prepare each area in more detail.

Look at the vocabulary and language you have in your textbooks and material you have from school, and take what you think might help you. Look also at the suggested structures in the vocabulary pages, and take a few you think will fit in with what you are going to say.

(a) Once you have chosen the kinds of thing you are going to say, consider the first section. You might decide to talk about how you got to your penpal's house. This will allow you to use the past tense, to describe your journey. You can fit in time and place words and phrases. You will also be able to use the vocabulary you know for methods of transport, and give your opinions on these. You can also introduce a couple of good structures, to show you know lots of good French! Here is an example of the kind of thing you can say:

> *L'année dernière je suis allé chez mon corres, qui habite en France. Je suis allé avec mon école: notre prof de français nous a accompagnés. Le voyage était très long, car on a pris le car de Glasgow à Douvres, puis le ferry de Douvres à Calais. En France, le voyage a duré six heures! Quel long voyage! Mais le voyage était quand même super, parce que j'étais avec mes amis, et on a écouté de la musique et regardé des cassettes vidéo dans le car!*

This would take about half a minute to say, and you would be working at Credit level. You could shorten it and simplify it, so that it would take 15 to 20 seconds, and you would still be working at General level. Once you have produced the first part, choose what will be your key words to help you when you carry out your presentation: this could be the first few words of your talk, to get you started, or key words from throughout the different sections, or a phrase which you always find hard to remember exactly. What is important is that it helps you remember your talk better.

(b) The second section could be about the school that your penpal goes to: this paragraph can be in the present tense, and allows you to compare a French school to your own school, and to give opinions. Look at the vocabulary given below, and try to put together your own paragraph. Make sure you put in some opinions and comparisons!

Il y a une bibliothèque et une cantine.	*There is a library and dinner hall*
Chez eux, on a le droit de ...	*They are allowed to ...*
Chez nous, on a le droit de ...	*We are allowed to ...*
On n'a pas le droit de ...	*They are not allowed to ...*
Il y a ... élèves et ... professeurs.	*There are ... pupils and ... teachers*
On ne porte pas l'uniforme scolaire	*You don't (have to) wear a school uniform*
Les cours commencent à ... et finit à ...	*Classes start at ... and finish at ...*
C'est un grand bâtiment moderne	*It is a large modern building*
C'est un collège mixte	*It is a mixed school*

When you are doing this, remember not to produce a list of things the school has, and to try to vary the language. Here is an example of what you could say:

Le collège de mon corres, qui s'appelle le Collège Victor Hugo, est un petit bâtiment gris au centre-ville. Chez eux, il y a une petite cantine, qui est beaucoup plus petite que chez nous. Il y a 600 élèves et 49 profs dans le collège. Les cours commencent à 8h30 tous les jours. On ne porte pas l'uniforme scolaire chez eux, et je trouve bizarre que tous les élèves arrivent en jean et baskets.

(c) Finally, you could prepare a section on your penpal's home town and family. Here are some words and phrases that you could work from.

Il y a (cinq) personnes dans sa famille	*There are (five) people in his family*
Il a des frères et des sœurs	*He has brothers and sisters*
Il n'a pas de frères/sœurs	*He doesn't have any brothers/sisters*
ses parents, son père, sa mère	*his/her parents, his/her father, his/her mother*
Ses parents sont très sympas	*His/her parents are very nice*
Je m'entends bien avec sa mère	*I get on well with his/her mum*
Sa ville est située dans le nord	*His/her town is in the north*
C'est une ville moyenne	*It's a middle-sized town*
à 50 kilomètres de Paris	*50 kilometres (30 miles) from Paris*
Il y a beaucoup à faire chez lui/chez elle	*There's lots of things to do in his/her town*

This last section is also very much in the present tense, but in the sample answer we have finished off with a different tense, the conditional. It also allows us to use the third person, varying our structures.

> *Mon corres habite avec ses parents et sa sœur dans une maison au centre-ville. Il n'a pas de frères, mais sa sœur est très sympa. Je m'entends très bien avec toute la famille. La ville est située dans le nord-est de la France, à 150 kilomètres de Paris. C'est une ville industrielle, mais aussi très agréable. Il y a beaucoup plus à faire chez lui que chez nous! Je voudrais y retourner l'année prochaine.*

2 Manger sain!

This topic will allow you to talk in the third person, use lots of opinion words and use good phrases from the texts that you are working from, so your first task should be to look at your source texts and select some bits. Then, break your task into areas. You could use a section in which you talk about what young people in Scotland actually eat, then have a section in which you talk about the dangers of fast-food and bad eating habits, and finish off with what you think people should do. If you have some material on what people eat in France, you could use this as well as, or instead of, the ideas above.

(a) The first section might sound something like this:

> *Chez nous on mange beaucoup de bonbons, de fast-food, et il semble que les Écossais aiment manger les pommes frites avec chaque repas. Beaucoup de jeunes ne prennent pas de petit déjeuner et arrivent au collège avec un Mars et une boîte de coca. On ne mange pas beaucoup de fruits et de légumes, et l'idée de cinq portions par jour ne semble pas réussir chez nous.*

(b) The second section is where you put in your longer sentences, while explaining what the dangers are:

> *Il est malsain de sortir le matin sans petit déjeuner, car sans nourriture on ne peut pas bien travailler à l'école: on ne peut pas se concentrer et apprendre. Manger trop de graisse aussi est dangereux, parce que la mauvaise nourriture peut encourager les maladies. Quand on ne mange pas assez de fruits et de légumes, il y a aussi des problèmes avec les dents, donc il faut visiter plus souvent le dentiste.*

(c) In this section you have the chance to show off all your ways of expressing opinions and making demands:

> *Il faut changer ce que les jeunes Écossais mangent. Nous ne devons pas accepter que les marchands de fast-food et de malbouffe vendent leurs produits dans nos cantines. Je le trouve indéfendable que cette possibilité existe. On doit*

défendre aux écoles de permettre les machines qui contiennent les boissons gazeux et des barres de chocolat. Nous devons encourager aux jeunes de penser à leur avenir, et d'adopter de bonnes habitudes à l'école.

3 Mon école

This is a tricky topic to choose, as it is very easy to produce too simple a piece of French on the subject. It can also be tempting to go for lists of subjects and teachers, which is a bad idea. So it is very important that you choose areas which will allow you to use a variety of structures, and also to use your vocabulary. When choosing sections, you might go for what you like and what you don't like at school: this allows you to give opinions and explanations. The final section could be a wish list of things you would like to see happen in your school in the future. This also allows you to use different tenses, including the future and the conditional. Here is the kind of thing you might say:

Il y a une chose que je n'aime pas chez mon collège: ce sont les devoirs. Lorsque je rentre à la maison, j'ai du travail pour deux heures chaque soir: je dois écrire des compositions anglaises, apprendre mes verbes français, et bien sûr faire les maths! En plus, je dois réviser pour mes examens, et je n'ai pas le temps de sortir avec mes amis.

En général, quand même, j'aime bien mon école: j'ai beaucoup de copains et de copines et je m'entends bien avec tout le monde, même les professeurs. Dans la récré et à midi on parle et rigole ensemble, et souvent dans la pause déjeuner nous allons en ville pour faire les magasins, parce que le collège est situé à seulement 400 mètres du centre-ville.

Mais, il y a une chose que j'aimerais changer: nous n'avons pas une salle où les élèves peuvent se réunir et bavarder. Il y a un échange entre notre collège et un collège en France, et chez eux ils ont une grande salle avec de la musique: ils peuvent y aller quand ils n'ont pas de classe. Je voudrais installer une salle de réunion chez nous aussi!

Grade-related criteria for Speaking: Prepared talk

Although short talks (of up to one minute) may be the norm in performances at Foundation level, longer talks may be the norm at General and Credit levels (up to a maximum of two minutes).

Foundation	General	Credit
◆ Talks are limited and may be unfocused or lacking in structure	◆ Talks go beyond basic content and show evidence of structure and/or focus	◆ Talks are comprehensive in content, well structured and/or focused
Candidates: ◆ can make a short presentation on a prepared topic ◆ can make themselves understood, although there may be mispronunciation, incorrect intonation, other-tongue interference, hesitation and quite frequent grammatical error ◆ have a limited range of vocabulary, structures and phrases ◆ tend to repeat structures and/or whole phrases ◆ may express simple opinions	**Candidates:** ◆ can speak at some length on a prepared topic ◆ can communicate with some success and accuracy in basic structures, although there may be some mispronunciation and weakness in intonation, grammatical errors and occasional hesitation ◆ may attempt a range of tenses and/or vocabulary ◆ can express opinions and reasons as required ◆ may make an attempt at a wider range of vocabulary, phrases and structures with frequent error, or may speak carefully and deliberately but be more accurate	**Candidates:** ◆ can make a full and comprehensive presentation on a prepared topic ◆ have no difficulty making themselves understood ◆ can use the language flexibly and are generally accurate although there may be occasional grammatical errors particularly in more complex language ◆ express opinions and reasons well and may expand on them ◆ have generally correct intonation and pronunciation

Grade 6	Grade 5	Grade 4	Grade 3	Grade 2	Grade 1
Talks tend to be short, limited in range, unfocused and very inaccurate	Talks may be short and limited in range, but are more focused and accurate	Talks may be inaccurate with reasonable range, or more accurate but lacking in range	Talks are more accurate and vocabulary and structures are more wide-ranging	Talks are mostly accurate but ideas are less well developed, or ideas are better developed but talks are less accurate	Candidates are able to speak at some length, showing both development of ideas and control of the language

The conversation

Preparing for the conversation is not really very different from preparing for the solo talk: you will know what topic area you are going to discuss, and you will make sure you have answers ready for whatever topic area you wish to discuss. You will not need to remember a big piece of text, but you will have to recognise which question needs which answer! You can also ask your own questions, and you should be ready to deal with the unexpected: this is not as difficult as it sounds, as there is a set of things you can do to help yourself.

The first thing you need to know are the question words, so you know what is being asked of you. Here are the main ones you will meet:

Qui…? *or* Qui est-ce que…?	*Who…?*
Qu'est-ce que…? *or* Qu'est-ce qui…?	*What…?*
Quand…? *or* Quand est-ce que…?	*When…?*
Où…? *or* Où est-ce que…?	*Where…?*
Quel…? *or* Quelle…?	*Which…?*
Pourquoi…? *or* Pourquoi est-ce que…?	*Why…?*
Comment…? *or* Comment est-ce que…?	*How…?*
Combien…?	*How much…? How many…?*

Remember that in English we use 'Do' to make a question: Do you have, Do you know, and so on. In French this will normally be done with *Est-ce que: Est-ce que tu as…? Est-ce qu tu sais…?* Let us look at making up questions. There are three main ways to do this.

1   Start with a question word if you need one. Add 'est-ce que'. Then carry on with subject and verb as in a normal sentence. For example, *Où est-ce que tu es allé?*

2   Another way to ask a question is just to change the way you say a sentence, by making your voice rise at the end (**intonation**). For example, *Tu aimes le fromage?*

3   The third method is **inversion**. That is, changing the order of the subject and the object: *As-tu…? Avez-vous…? For example, As-tu un frère?*

What else do we have to think about? As for the prepared talk, your teacher will assess you using the grade-related criteria, which are given on p. 67. You should look at the level you are aiming for, and then make sure you show that you can do the things you need to do. Think about what the criteria mean. Here are some of them from the Credit list:

Candidates:	What you need to do
◆ readily take initiative	This means you should ask questions too, or change the subject
◆ express agreement, disagreement, opinions and reasons well and can expand on them if required	Remember to give opinions, and reasons for them
◆ have no difficulty making themselves understood and can use the language flexibly, coping well with unexpected questions	Be ready to say, *Pardon, je n'ai pas compris, Voulez-vous répéter, s'il vous plaît?* to give you time to think
◆ are generally accurate although there may be occasional grammatical errors and weaknesses in pronunciation	Make sure your preparation gives you lots of good material, which you have checked and learned in advance
◆ speak with little hesitation, other-tongue interference or weakness in intonation	Being prepared is all-important!
◆ can use a range of language structures with some confidence	Make sure you have good structures prepared for your answers
◆ may attempt a range of tenses	Think about tenses when preparing your answers!

Let us look at the topic *Manger sain*, which was used on pp. 61–62 to demonstrate a solo talk. On p. 66 is a list of possible questions you might be faced with in a conversation on the same topic. There are different ways of asking questions, but that won't affect your answers. Try to put your own answers to the questions, using the vocabulary you know from studying this area, and remembering to refer to pages 79–80, where you will find guidelines on giving your opinion. Then have a look at the sample answers. Remember this is a conversation, so you should be ready to ask some of these questions yourself. You can either just ask them, or, if you have just been asked one, after your answer, say *Et toi?* or *Et vous?,* then repeat the question.

If your teacher is playing the part of a young person, or your test is with another student, use *tu*: however, if your test is with an adult, remember to use *Et vous?* and change also the form of the question. You will find more help on asking questions with *vous* in the role-play section, starting on p. 69.

Est-ce que ta santé est importante pour toi?

Pourquoi?

Comment est-ce que tu trouves les repas à la cantine du collège?

Ta famille aime manger sain?

Comment trouves-tu les plats végétariens?

Qu'est-ce que tu fais pour garder ta forme?

Qu'est-ce que tu manges au petit déjeuner normalement?

Qu'est-ce que tu bois avec ton déjeuner?

Combien de bonbons est-ce que tu achètes chaque semaine?

Qu'est-ce que tu as mangé/bu à midi?

Questions	Sample answers
Est-ce que ta santé est importante pour toi?	*Oui, elle est très importante pour moi.*
Pourquoi? (What you will be asked if you just say 'oui' to the previous question)	*Parce que je n'aime pas être malade, et je suis aussi très sportif/sportive.*
Comment est-ce que tu trouves les repas à la cantine du collège? (Whatever your answer, try to say at least two things)	*Je les trouve affreux: je n'aime pas du tout manger à la cantine.*
Ta famille aime manger sain? (Again, two things at least: you could include yourself in the answer as well)	*Mes parents aiment manger sain, mais mes sœurs préfèrent les hamburgers.*
Comment trouves-tu les plats végétariens? (Allows a different tense)	*Je n'aimerais pas devenir végétarien(ne), parce que j'aime trop la viande.*
Qu'est-ce que tu fais pour garder ta forme? (A chance to say lots here)	*Je fais du sport trois fois par semaine, je mange bien, et je me couche tôt.*
Qu'est-ce que tu manges au petit déjeuner normalement? (Again, say lots, but don't use lists)	*Normalement, je prends des céréales avec du lait, et du fruit.*
Qu'est-ce que tu bois avec ton déjeuner? (Use the opportunity to put in an opinion)	*Je ne bois jamais de coca: je préfère boire de l'eau ou du thé.*
Combien de bonbons est-ce que tu achètes chaque semaine? (A past tense)	*Je n'achète plus les bonbons: j'ai renoncé il y a six mois.*
Qu'est-ce que tu as mangé/bu à midi? (Again lots of potential: watch lists!)	*J'ai mangé un sandwich et du fruit en ville, avec mes copains.*

Grade-related criteria for Speaking: Conversation and Role-play

Although short conversations with the interlocutor (speaking partner) of up to two minutes may be the norm in performances at Foundation level, longer conversations should be the norm at General and Credit levels (up to a maximum of five minutes).

Foundation	General	Credit
The interlocutor:	**The interlocutor:**	**The interlocutor:**
◆ uses short phrases and sentences	◆ goes beyond short phrases and sentences	◆ can use a wide range of language
◆ has to speak slowly, perhaps using repetition and/or rephrasing	◆ can usually speak at normal speed, using repetition and/or rephrasing as required	◆ can speak at normal speed, occasionally using repetition and/or rephrasing
◆ has to provide a great deal of (unsolicited) help	◆ has to provide some help	◆ may have to provide minimal help
Candidates:	**Candidates:**	**Candidates:**
◆ can take part in simple conversations	◆ can take part in simple conversations	◆ can take part in extended conversations
◆ can ask for help, and with help provided can understand most of what is said	◆ can understand most of what is said and can ask for help if required	◆ can understand immediately almost everything said and seldom need to ask for help
◆ tend to limit themselves to basic content and phrases	◆ are prepared to go beyond basic content and phrases	◆ have no difficulty going beyond basic content and phrases
◆ may express simple opinions	◆ may take the initiative	◆ readily take initiative
◆ can make themselves understood	◆ can express agreement, disagreement, opinions and reasons	◆ express agreement, disagreement, opinions and reasons well and can expand on them if required
◆ beyond fixed phrases, the language tends to be inaccurate and hesitant, with mispronunciation, incorrect intonation, other-tongue interference and frequent grammatical errors	◆ can communicate with some success and cope reasonably well with unexpected questions, although there may be many grammatical errors	◆ have no difficulty making themselves understood and can use the language flexibly, coping well with unexpected questions
◆ have a limited range of vocabulary and structures	◆ there may be mispronunciation, occasional other-tongue interference and weakness in intonation	◆ are generally accurate although there may be occasional grammatical errors and weaknesses in pronunciation
	◆ may speak carefully and deliberately with some accuracy, or be more fluent but less accurate	◆ speak with little hesitation, other-tongue interference or weakness in intonation
	◆ show a reasonable range of vocabulary and structures	◆ can use a range of language structures with some confidence
	◆ may attempt a range of tenses	◆ may attempt a range of tenses

This is how a particular grade will be decided:

Foundation		General		Credit	
Grade 6	Grade 5	Grade 4	Grade 3	Grade 2	Grade 1
Interactions tend to be very limited in range. Candidates need a lot of unsolicited help	Interactions are less limited in range and content. Candidates need some unsolicited help	Interactions may be inaccurate with reasonable range, or more accurate but lacking in range	Interactions are more accurate and vocabulary and structures are more wide-ranging	Interactions are mostly accurate and candidate is able to use the language flexibly	Candidates are able to converse at some length and show control of the language

The role-play

This requires polite, formal language (the kind of language you might find in a transaction, a job interview and in a vocational situation). You must also use *vous, votre,* and the verb forms that go with *vous.* If it is a **transaction**, then it will be straightforward to prepare for this, as the task will be structured, and you will know what you are expected to ask and can prepare this thoroughly. In a **vocational** situation, where the task will be more conversational, you should also follow the guidance given for the conversation type of assessment.

In this section, we will take you through preparing for both these types of role-play. However, remember that most of the advice in the conversation guidelines applies to this assessment as well, and make sure you have checked out the support on forming questions.

A transactional task

We will look at one kind of transactional task; the techniques and much of the advice here can be carried over to other tasks, however. This task is very straightforward, but it is one where the teacher might try to make things awkward, to allow you to 'negotiate', and deal with the unexpected.

Booking a hotel

You are intending to go to France with your family on holiday: you phone a hotel to try to book accommodation. Your teacher will play the part of the person at the hotel. You should know how much you want to pay before you start, and what accommodation you are looking for!

You should carry out the following tasks:

◆ Ask if they have rooms available in July

◆ Ask if they have rooms with a bath/shower

◆ Give some dates, and ask if the rooms are available then

◆ Find out if there is a restaurant

◆ Ask the cost for: (a) rooms (b) breakfast

◆ Ask when breakfast will be served

◆ Ask if they have rooms with a balcony

◆ Ask where exactly the hotel is.

Task	What you need to do
◆ Ask if they have rooms available in July	Remember to start off by introducing yourself, and saying why you are calling: *Bonjour, je m'appelle ... je vous téléphone pour ...* Be prepared to have to spell your name. You should also know how many rooms you want: *Je cherche deux chambres pour ...*
◆ Ask if they have rooms with a bath/shower	Remember you must keep on using 'vous', and to use the correct question form: e.g. *Est-ce que vous avez...?* You may be given an option in the answer, such as a price difference, and you should be ready for this!
◆ Give some dates, and ask if the rooms are available then	This gives you a chance to put in a different tense, the conditional. *Nous voudrions arriver le ... et rester jusqu'au ... Est-ce que vous auriez des chambres pour ces dates?* Again, be ready to accept different dates, if the teacher offers them, or to ask for an alternative: *Oui, ce serait possible pour nous./Non, ce ne serait pas possible: est-ce que nous pourrions arriver le ...*
◆ Find out if there is a restaurant	Vary the way you ask questions: just use intonation for this one: *Il y a un restaurant à l'hôtel?*

continues overleaf

Task	What you need to do
◆ Ask the cost for: (a) rooms (b) breakfast	There are lots of ways of asking how much something costs: to vary it, you can just ask if breakfast is included: *Deux chambres avec... ça coûte combien? Le petit déjeuner est compris dans le prix?* To make your conversation better, repeat the answer and write down the costs. And remember your budget: you might have to ask for cheaper rooms, if the prices you are quoted are too high! *Vous avez des chambres moins chères?*
◆ Ask when breakfast will be served	A straightforward question! *À quelle heure est-ce que le petit déjeuner est servi?* To make your conversation better, repeat the answer and write down the times.
◆ Ask if they have rooms with a balcony	Try a different form of question, using inversion. *Avez-vous des chambres avec balcon?*
◆ Ask where exactly the hotel is	Again, a straightforward question, and a chance to note down the answer. *Où se trouve l'hôtel exactement?* And, finally, remember to finish off the booking. You could say you will call back to confirm the booking: *Je vous téléphonerai demain pour confirmer.*

A vocational role-play

You have an interview for a job as a waiter in France for the summer. Your teacher will play the role of interviewer. This is a chance for you to give longer answers for a Credit grade, or more straightforward answers for a General grade. You should also use the chance to ask some questions. Some suggestions are added below, but make up more if you feel confident!

Questions	Some suggestions
Comment vous appelez-vous?	Remember to start off by saying Hello! You could also add in your nationality and the answer to the next question. *Bonjour, monsieur/madam. Je m'appelle ... Je suis écossais(e)*
Comment ça s'écrit?	Know your alphabet!
Quel âge avez-vous?	You could also add in the answer to the next question. *J'ai ... ans. Je suis né(e) le ...*

Questions	Some suggestions
Votre lieu et date de naissance?	Straightforward, and the chance to add your nationality, if you have not already done so. *Je suis né(e) le ... à ...*
Vous habitez où?	You can add the details about where you live, where exactly it is, and your address if you want! *J'habite ... en ... C'est dans le ... Mon adresse, c'est ...*
Quel poste voulez-vous?	You know the job, because it is in the instructions. You can add in the bit about your experience here, if you want to extend your answer. *Je cherche un poste comme serveur/serveuse ...*
Vous avez de l'expérience?	A chance to give details, if you wish: where you worked, how long for, what you thought of it, and so on. *Oui, j'ai déjà travaillé comme ... chez ... J'ai travaillé pendant ... ans. J'aimais bien mon travail ...*
Quelles langues parlez-vous?	Don't just give a list: say how well you speak them, and how long you have learned them for: *Je parle couramment/un peu le ... Je l'apprends depuis ...*
Vous avez un petit boulot?	Another chance to give details, if you wish: where you work, how long for, and so on. *Oui, je travaille comme ... chez ... J'ai travaillé pendant ... ans. J'aime bien mon travail ...*
Quelles sont vos qualités personnelles?	A chance to say nice things about yourself! *Je suis travailleur/-euse, honnête, et je m'entends bien avec tout le monde!*
Quand est-ce que vous pouvez commencer?	A chance to answer the next question at the same time. *Je pourrais commencer le ... Je veux rester*
Vous voulez rester combien de temps?	*Je veux rester jusqu'au ... Est-ce que cela vous convient?*
Vous avez des questions?	A chance for you to ask some questions. *Est-ce que je peux loger dans l'hôtel? Combien d'heures est-ce qu'on doit travailler? Il y a beaucoup de travail le week-end? Combien est-ce que je vais gagner?*
	Remember to say Goodbye properly! *Alors merci, et au revoir, monsieur/madame.*

WRITING

Writing is worth **one-sixth** of your overall Standard Grade result. You will have to carry out at least three writing assessments during your course, for a folio of work: the subjects of these pieces of writing will be set by your teacher in discussion with you, and you can draft and redraft following advice from your teacher. You can use textbooks and work you have already produced to guide you in your preparation, and you can work from guidelines provided by your teacher. This means you can really plan out what you want to write.

The pieces must be written under controlled conditions finally, with only a dictionary and your memory to help you. You will have 30 minutes under exam conditions to produce each final piece of writing. The folio of three pieces will be sent to SQA for marking. However, you have a lot of control over what is in your folio, and you may have more than three pieces from which you and your teacher select the best. The SQA will take the marks for your three tests and make an average of them: this will be your final writing grade.

The rules for the assessments are very open: you can write in a whole variety of different styles, and there are no kinds of writing you *must* do. You might find that the topics you are using for your speaking assessments will also do for your writing assessments, which could save you a lot of time and effort. Your writing will be graded according to how well it demonstrates a sense of structure, control of grammar, focus on the task and communication. The way of judging how well you have done is given in the grade-related criteria for writing: these are shown opposite, so that you can see what is expected of you.

Grade-related criteria for Writing

These criteria are to be understood as characteristics of writing at each level; thus, for example, the length of a piece of writing or its accuracy alone is not sufficient to guarantee an award at a particular level. The **overall quality** of the written language is what is being assessed.

Foundation	General	Credit
◆ the content is appropriate to the task, but very limited ◆ communication is achieved despite frequent grammatical errors ◆ candidates may express simple opinions ◆ candidates can use simple structures with some accuracy ◆ there is a limited range of vocabulary and structures ◆ there may be a tendency to repeat structures and/or phrases	◆ writing shows evidence of structure and/or focus ◆ communication is achieved with some success and consistency, despite grammatical errors ◆ candidates can express simple opinions and reasons ◆ candidates can use simple structures with more accuracy ◆ there is a reasonable range of vocabulary and structures ◆ there may be an attempt at a range of tenses	◆ writing is well structured and/or focused ◆ candidates can write with some flexibility ◆ candidates can express opinions and reasons well and may expand on them ◆ candidates are generally accurate in their use of language although there may be occasional grammatical errors, particularly in more complex structures ◆ there is evidence of a wide range of vocabulary and structures ◆ candidates use a range of tenses as appropriate

Grade 6	Grade 5	Grade 4	Grade 3	Grade 2	Grade 1
Writing is limited in range and very inaccurate	Writing is limited in range, but may be more focused and/or accurate	Writing may be inaccurate but with a reasonable range, or more accurate but lacking in range	Writing is more accurate, and vocabulary and structures are more wide-ranging	Writing is mostly accurate but ideas are less well developed or ideas are better developed but writing is less accurate	Candidates are able to write at some length showing both development of ideas and control of the language

For a Foundation award, about 25 words are needed in each piece. For a General award, you should be able to write 50 words or more. For a Credit award, you need 100 words or more for each piece. Normally you will need at least the minimum number of words to be able to show that you have a command of the structures and vocabulary necessary to demonstrate you are working at that level.

However, what will be more important than the word count is your accuracy and sense of structure. We will look at how you can show this in the next pages. For a Foundation award, it is important to write as accurately as you can! To get a General award, you will have to try to use a variety of tenses and structures. You should be able to give your opinions on what you are writing about, and try to be as accurate as you can. Your writing should always focus on the topic you have chosen.

For Credit, you will have to use more complex and sophisticated language. You must be reasonably accurate in your use of French, and use tenses well. Your opinions will be more important than at General level, and you should also include reasons for some of these opinions. Your writing will have to be more varied and flexible!

Planning your writing

Once you've chosen your topic area, focus on the actual language that you will use. Try to look at two or three headings, to break the task down for you. Preparing a writing assessment is very like preparing a prepared talk. The do's and don'ts are very similar.

Do's

◆ Do look at the textbook or texts you are working from for good ideas you can use.

◆ Do make sure you understand what you are writing, or it will be very difficult to remember it properly when you have to do the final writing for the folio.

◆ Do show a draft to your teacher, to get any suggestions, or so that you can make corrections.

◆ Do write on every second line, to make it easier to put in changes and corrections.

◆ Do use a variety of structures: use different tenses, use joining words like *parce que* or *quand* to make longer sentences, use adjectives, adverbs and phrases that you know are correct.

◆ Do give your opinion, and work at having different ways of saying what you think. Look at the 'Giving opinions' section on pp. 79–80.

WRITING

Don'ts

◆ Don't leave the preparation to the last minute! If you start your preparation early, you'll be able to ask your teacher for advice on any vocabulary or grammar you're unsure of.

◆ Don't always stick to safe, simple language. It may be easier, but won't get the best grades. Try out some of the more impressive sentences you've learned. Note down useful vocabulary and phrases you've seen elsewhere under appropriate topic headings so you can reuse them in your writing assessments.

◆ Don't use lists of things as these will not help you to show structure or knowledge of French. What will be more important than the actual number of words is the number and variety of structures.

To help you prepare for a writing assessment, we have selected two possible topics, one using **personal** language, and the other using **discursive** language. We will guide you through the process of preparing for and carrying out the assessment: you can follow the same pattern, for a topic of your own choice, and you might also find Chapter 10 on speaking useful to prepare for a specific writing task.

1 **A letter to a French-speaking friend**
2 *La télévision*

1 Personal language

A letter to a French-speaking friend

You decide to write a letter to a friend in French. Sort out your ideas and choose the areas you feel most confident about – best of all, the areas you have been covering in class recently. Think about ways of getting different tenses and structures into your writing. Plan what you are going to write. We will imagine here that you are going to write about your family.

Look at the vocabulary in Chapter 12, and take what you think might help you. Look also at the suggested structures, and take a few you think will fit in with what you are going to say.

Now that you have chosen the kinds of thing that you are going to say, let us look at the first section. After you start off the letter with some letter-writing vocabulary, you are going to describe who is in your family. This lets you start off with simple language, which you should make sure is correct. You can fit in adjectives, and verbs with *il* and *elle*. You will also be able to use any special phrases you know. You can also introduce a couple of good structures, to show you know lots of good French! Here is an example of the kind of thing you can say:

Salut, Pierre,

Ça va? Ici, tout va bien. Tu m'as demandé de te raconter un peu de ma famille. Chez nous, il y a mon père, Lewis, et ma mère Helen, et mes deux frères. Mon père, il a 38 ans, et il a les cheveux bruns et courts. Helen, ma mère, est petite et mince.

This is about 50 words, and would be a start to producing a piece of writing at Credit level: add another couple of sentences, and you have a piece of writing at General level. For General, the following would fit the criteria:

Mon père travaillait comme facteur, mais maintenant il a un poste dans un bureau. Ma mère n'a jamais travaillé, car elle a trois enfants! Et comment est ta famille?

Au revoir,

The second section for Credit level could go on to talk about how you get on with your parents: this paragraph can include a past tense, and allows you to give opinions. Here is an example of what you could write:

Je m'entends bien avec mon père, parce que nous aimons tous les deux le football, et aussi parce qu'il me donne mon argent de poche! J'ai toujours aimé ma mère, parce qu'elle m'aidait beaucoup quand j'avais des problèmes à l'école.

This adds roughly another 40 words to your writing, and shows a variety of tenses and structures. Finally, you could prepare a section on a problem that you have, to get more variety in. This is the kind of thing you might write:

Mon seul problème est que je n'ai pas assez de liberté: mes parents n'aiment pas quand je sors le soir et le week-end, ils préfèrent que je reste à la maison! Quelle barbe! Alors, je vais écrire de mon école la prochaine fois: et toi, comment est ta famille?

Au revoir,

These three paragraphs make up about 130 words, which is right for Credit level, and also gives you a variety of structures. You need to be able to understand what you have written so you can remember it when you actually have to do the folio piece of writing: so follow the golden rules:

1   Make sure you choose words you are familiar with.

2   Make sure you know it's correct.

3   Have a variety of tenses and structures in there.

4   Do the proof-reading when you have finished!

2 Discursive writing

La télévision

This style of writing will allow you to write about a topic, use lots of opinion words and use good phrases from the texts that you are working from, so your first task should be to look at your source texts and select some bits. Then, break your task into areas. For a Foundation award, you could write a section about what you watch. For a General award, you could start with a section about what you watch, then go on to talk about your favourite programme. For Credit, you could use a section in which you talk about what you watch, then have a section in which you talk about what other young people in your class watch (allowing you to put in third person verbs), and finish off writing about the dangers of too much TV and not enough exercise.

The first section might read something like this:

Je ne regarde pas beaucoup la télé, car je n'ai pas le temps après le sport et mes devoirs. Je regarde un feuilleton tous les soirs avant de dîner, et le week-end je regarde quelquefois du foot ou un film.

This is about 40 words. The second section could be either of these two:

(General) *Mon programme favori, c'est une série américaine qui s'appelle 'Buffy contre les vampires'. J'ai toujours regardé Buffy, car j'adore Sarah Michelle Gellar, l'actrice qui joue Buffy!*

This gives you a total of almost 70 words, and has a past tense in it as well as an opinion and a reason.

(Credit) *Mes copains aussi ne regardent pas beaucoup la télé, mais bien sûr nous avons tous passé des heures devant la télé quand nous étions plus jeunes. On regardait tous les feuilletons et on en a discuté le lendemain à l'école.*

You have the chance to demonstrate a variety of tenses and verb structures here, and show that you have a good knowledge of more than the basics! The final section gives you the chance to show ways of expressing opinions and giving reasons for your opinions:

Il faut penser aux dangers pour les jeunes de regarder trop la télé. Nous savons déjà que nous jeunes mangent trop de fast-food. Je le trouve dangéreux de combiner le fast-food avec une manque d'exercice. Nous devons encourager aux jeunes de penser à leur santé, sinon nous aurons de grands problèmes dans le futur!

Once you have written your first draft, had it corrected, and have a good version which you are going to learn for the day of the actual assessment, how can you go about learning it? There are various things you can try.

First, if at all possible, produce your writing as a word-processed document: this makes it easier to change, draft and redraft! You can then take that document and make a new copy with every second word blanked out, to help you remember what you wrote the first time. You can then go to a version which only has a few key words left, as a guideline to writing out the text again.

You might find it helpful just to write out the document several times. Each time you do so, compare it carefully with the original, to make sure you are not putting in errors. This is called proof-reading, and is an essential part of the task!

Get somebody to help you, if you can: they can hold the original text, and give you clue words when you need them, as you try to remember what you have written.

Finally, on the day of the assessment, remember you are only allowed a dictionary and your memory. You will have 30 minutes to produce the writing, but you should not need all this time if you are prepared. You should not be using your dictionary at this stage to look up any new words, as this might introduce new errors! Instead, use it as you go along, and after you have finished, to check what you have written for accuracy. Remember also to look at your verb endings, as the accuracy of these will have a big influence on what grade you are awarded.

The most important factor in getting a good writing grade is preparation: make sure you research your first draft, have it corrected, and have your final working draft checked and correct. This all takes time, so make sure you start early!

STRUCTURES AND VOCABULARY

To help you in both speaking and writing, this chapter should act as a reference when producing your own work. As you may see when you look at the grade-related criteria in Chapters 10 and 11, you will be assessed in both skills on your use of structure, your use of opinions and reasons, your use of a variety of grammatical structures and tenses, as well as (of course) the accuracy of your writing and speaking! You should try to make sure that your preparation for writing and speaking works towards these criteria.

Structure

Good structure means that your work is directly related to the topic that you are writing or speaking about. You should not just collect a whole set of different phrases and sentences, and jumble them all together. Best of all is the structure where you introduce the topic, give your opinions and come to a conclusion. If you are talking about school, you should not have a whole lot of material about where you live, how old you are, and your family. This is irrelevant! You should also avoid the temptation to give long lists: when talking about sport, for instance, do not simply give a list of sports you do, and when talking about television, avoid a list of your favourite programmes. If you write a letter, start and finish it properly.

Giving opinions

You might find the following phrases useful in giving your opinions:

J'aime, j'adore, je préfère	*I like, love, prefer*
Je n'aime pas, je déteste	*I don't like, I hate*
J'ai horreur de ...	*I really hate*
Je trouve que c'est ...	*I think that it's ...*
Je trouve cela formidable	*I find that terrific*
Je le trouve bête que ...	*I find it stupid that ...*
C'est fantastique, très bien, génial, intéressant, passionnant, marrant	*It's fantastic, very good, great, interesting, exciting, fun*

C'est minable, triste, déprimant, pénible, nul, ennuyeux	*It's awful, sad, depressing, terrible, rubbish, boring*
C'est mieux/pire de ...	*It is better/worse to ...*
Il y a (Il y avait) trop de ...	*There is (There was) too much/many ...*
Il n'y a pas assez de ...	*There is not enough ...*
Il serait utile de pouvoir ...	*It would be useful to be able to ...*
À mon avis	*In my opinion*
Il faut penser à ...	*You have to think about ...*
Il ne faut pas oublier que ...	*We mustn't forget that ...*
Nous devons ... Nous ne devons pas ...	*We should ... We shouldn't ...*
J'aimerais savoir que ...	*I would like to know that ...*
Je voudrais voir ...	*I would like to see ...*

Giving reasons

Giving reasons for your opinions, or for why things happen, can be done by using conjunctions. This is a good idea, as it allows you to do two things at the same time: you are expressing yourself, and you are also using more complex structures and language. Conjunctions (joining words) are words like *car, parce que*, *donc*, which say why something is the way it is. Look at the sentences below to see them in action when discussing pocket money: first comes the statement, followed by a reason (or linked statement). Try to have at least two sentences like this in every piece of writing you do, and make sure you leave an opportunity for sentences like this in your preparation for speaking assessments.

Je n'ai jamais assez d'argent de poche, **car** j'achète trop de vêtements.	*I never have enough pocket money, **since/as** I buy too many clothes.*
J'adore les vendredis, **parce que** c'est là que je reçois mon argent de poche.	*I love Fridays, **because** that's when I get my pocket money.*
Je n'ai pas beaucoup d'argent de poche, **donc** il me faut travailler les samedis.	*I don't get a lot of pocket money, so I have to work on Saturdays.*

Grammatical variety

The marks you get for your speaking and writing assessments will be affected by the structures that you use. Sometimes this means using good phrases and sentences you know, but often it is just a question of making sure all your sentences do not start with *Je*. Make sure you create opportunities to use *nous* and *on* (remembering to get the verb ending right). Think about sentences in which you talk about what other people think or do. Here is a list of things you might consider putting into your preparation:

◆ attaching adjectives to nouns, with the correct endings, of course;

◆ using negatives with your verbs, putting the two words in the correct place;

◆ using pronouns in your sentences;

◆ using modal verbs: *Je **peux** aller ..., On **doit** savoir que ... Il **faut** ...*

Tenses

The final thing to think about is the use of a variety of tenses. Every speaking or writing task should use at least two different tenses. This means planning the tenses into your preparation. If you are discussing school, for instance, you could say what things used to be like, what will happen next year, or what you would like to happen. If you are discussing clothes, again you can say what you or other people used to wear, and what you are intending buying this weekend!

For the purpose of preparing for Standard Grade assessments, we can divide the tenses into three: present, past and future. Let us look at each of these three.

The present

The present tense only has one form, but you can expand on this by using modal verbs or auxiliaries: here are some examples of this:

Je veux travailler le week-end	*I want to work at the weekend*
On ne peut pas faire beaucoup chez nous	*You can't do a lot where we live*
Il faut aller à Glasgow pour voir un film	*You have to go to Glasgow to see a film*
Je dois faire beaucoup à la maison	*I have to do a lot at home*

The past

You should be able to use two tenses in the past: these tenses have various names, although most books refer to them as the **perfect** and the **imperfect**. You should use the perfect to talk about an event in the past, and the imperfect to describe how things used to be. If your whole assessment is based on the past, then you should use both tenses. If most of what you are discussing is in the present, then put in one or both of these tenses as well. Here are some examples of the kind of thing you might say, when discussing your hobbies:

J'ai commencé de jouer au foot il y a quatre ans	*I started to play football four years ago*
Je jouais avec mes amis d'abord	*I used to play with my friends at first*
On a gagné la finale en 2004	*We won the final in 2004*
Je l'aimais beaucoup	*I used to like it a lot*

The future

There are three different ways to talk about the future that you should be able to use. However, this is not as frightening as it sounds, as much of it is very straightforward. You should be able to demonstrate the use of the informal future, the formal future and the conditional. Here are some examples of these, with sentences referring to your plans for the future.

The **informal future** is very easy: you just use the present tense of *aller*, together with the infinitive of the verb that you are using.

Je vais retourner à l'école l'année prochaine	*I'm coming back to school next year*
On va aller en vacances ensemble	*We're going to go on holiday together*
Mes parents vont payer mes vacances	*My parents are going to pay for my holiday*

The **formal future** is the tense where you do have to know your endings, and where there are irregular verb forms, but any good dictionary will let you find these out!

J'irai à l'université	*I will go to university*
J'habiterai chez mes parents	*I'll live with my parents*
Ma copine ira à Aberdeen	*My friend is going to go to Aberdeen*

The **conditional** tense is very like the formal future in its formation, but has slightly different endings. There are, however, some very straightforward phrases using the conditional, which would fit most pieces of writing. It talks about what *could* happen. Here are four examples, used to talk about your plans for the summer:

J'aimerais aller en Espagne	*I'd like to go to Spain*
Je voudrais aller avec mes amis	*I'd like to go with my friends*
Je ne travaillerais pas pendant les vacances	*I wouldn't work during the holidays*
Ça serait formidable!	*That would be great!*

Vocabulary

These pages are for your reference. When you are getting ready for a listening or reading test, you should check that you know the vocabulary in each topic area, and you can use the pages as a revision guide. When you have a writing or speaking task, use this vocabulary to help you with ideas. Each section has some starter sentences, but there is also space for you to add your own sentences and phrases: things that you know are correct and that you think will fit the task. Whenever you see a good phrase, just note it down and then write it in the space provided in each topic area.

These are the topic areas covered:

1 Using numbers (including times, dates, temperatures, distances and prices)

2 Days, months, weeks and years

3 Jobs and professions

4 School, including subjects studied

5 Food and drink

6 Family members

7 The weather and seasons

8 Hobbies and sports

9 House, daily routine and household tasks

10 Places in town

11 Modes of transport

1 Using numbers

Times

neuf heures	nine o'clock
neuf heures et quart	quarter past nine
neuf heures vingt	twenty past nine
neuf heures et demie	half past nine
neuf heures moins le quart	quarter to nine
neuf heures moins cinq	five to nine
midi et demi, minuit et demi	half past twelve

Remember that most official times in French use the 24-hour clock, and there is no use of 'am' or 'pm':

treize heures	1.00 pm (13:00)
dix-huit heures trente	6.30 pm (18:30)

Dates
Remember that all dates use cardinal numbers, except for 'the first':

le premier mai	May 1st
le deux mai	May 2nd
je suis né(e) le 14 octobre	I was born on October 14th

Temperatures
France, like most other countries in the world, uses centigrade to measure temperatures. So a weather forecast will say something like: *Aujourd'hui il fait quinze degrés*. Make sure you know your numbers!

Distances
Remember that you should never use measurements such as 'miles' when talking and writing in French, but always metres and kilometres:

Glasgow se trouve à 80 kilomètres d'Edimbourg	Glasgow is 80 km (50 miles) from Edinburgh
J'habite à 500 mètres de l'école	I live 500 metres (roughly a quarter of a mile) from school

Prices
Prices are all in euros and cents. (Old prices, in francs, are still shown in some books, but they will not feature in your exam.)

Un coca coûte trois euros. J'ai payé trois euros cinquante (€3,50).

When writing about money in the UK, you should use *un livre* for 'one pound':

Je gagne 20 livres tous les samedis au magasin.

Put your own phrases in the spaces below:

2 Days, weeks, months and years

lundi	Monday
mardi	Tuesday
mercredi	Wednesday
jeudi	Thursday
vendredi	Friday
samedi	Saturday
dimanche	Sunday
janvier	January
février	February
mars	March
avril	April
mai	May
juin	June
juillet	July
août	August
septembre	September
octobre	October
novembre	November
décembre	December
mercredi, le 25 novembre	Wednesday the 25th of November

le matin	morning
l'après-midi (m)	afternoon
le soir	evening
la nuit	night
un jour, une journée	a day
une semaine	a week
quinze jours	a fortnight
un mois	a month
un an	a year (used on its own or with a number)
j'ai quinze ans	I am 15
une année	a year (used with an adjective)
une bonne année	a good year
mille neuf cent quatre-vingt treize	1993

Put your own phrases in the spaces below:

3 Jobs and professions

Remember that when saying what someone does for a living, you don't need *un(e)* or *le/la*. For example: *Mon père est dentiste* (my father is a dentist).

acteur/actrice	actor/actress
agent de police	policeman/policewoman
agriculteur/agricultrice	farmer
avocat	lawyer
boucher/bouchère	butcher
boulanger/boulangère	baker
caissier/caissière	cashier, checkout operator
chauffeur de taxi	taxi driver

chômeur/chômeuse	unemployed person
coiffeur/coiffeuse	hairdresser, hair stylist
cuisinier/cuisinière	cook
directeur/directrice	headteacher, director
dentiste	dentist
électricien/électricienne	electrician
facteur/factrice	postman/woman
hôtesse de l'air	air hostess
jardinier/jardinière	gardener
journaliste	journalist
infirmier/infirmière	nurse
ingénieur	engineer
maçon	bricklayer, builder
mécanicien/mécanicienne	mechanic
médecin	doctor
patron/patronne	boss, owner
plombier	plumber
PDG (président-directeur général)	managing director, chief executive
professeur, prof	teacher
secrétaire	secretary
serveur/serveuse	waiter/waitress, barman
technicien/technicienne	technician
vendeur/vendeuse	shop/sales assistant

Starter sentences

Ma mère est professeur	My mum is a teacher
Je voudrais devenir infirmière	I'd like to be/become a nurse
Je vais aller en fac	I'm going to go to university
Je veux continuer mes études	I'm going to stay on at school/continue sixth year studies
Le samedi, je travaille dans un café	I work in a café on Saturdays
J'ai un petit boulot de vendeuse	I have a part-time job in a shop

Put your own phrases in the spaces below:

4 School subjects

l'allemand (m)	German
l'anglais (m)	English
la biologie	biology
la chimie	chemistry
le commerce	business studies
le dessin	art
l'EMT (f) (éducation manuelle et technique)	craft and design
l'EPS (f) (éducation physique et sportive)	PE
l'espagnol (m)	Spanish
le français	French
la géographie	geography
l'histoire (f)	history
l'informatique (f)	IT
les maths (m pl)	maths
la musique	music
la politique/l'instruction (f) civique	modern studies
la physique	physics
les sciences (f pl)	science
le sport	sport
la technologie	technological studies
le lundi, j'ai géo	On Mondays I have geography
j'aime les maths	I like maths

School (general)

le collège/le CES (collège d'enseignement secondaire)	secondary school (roughly S1–S4)
le lycée	secondary school (roughly S5–S6)
le bac/baccalauréat	(equivalent to Highers)
la bibliothèque	library
un bulletin	report
une cantine	canteen
un cours	lesson
les devoirs (m pl)	homework
un/une élève	pupil
les études (f pl)	study, schoolwork
un examen	exam
la fac/l'université (f)	uni/university
un laboratoire	laboratory
une matière	a subject
la pause de midi	lunchtime break
un professeur, un/une prof	teacher
la récréation/la récré	morning interval, break
une salle de classe	classroom
les vacances (f pl)	holidays
les grandes vacances	summer holidays
les vacances de Pâques/de Noël	Easter/Christmas holidays

Useful school adjectives

bête	stupid
chouette	great
difficile	difficult
dur(e)	hard
ennuyeux/ennuyeuse	boring
facile	easy
faible: je suis faible en …	not so good at
fort: je suis fort(e) en …	good at
intéressant(e)	interesting
marrant(e)	funny

89

nul: je suis nul en …	useless
passionnant(e)	exciting, great
sévère	strict
utile	useful

Remember that French pupils of about your age will talk about being in *quatrième (S3)* and then *troisième (S4)*, because in France the secondary years start with 'sixth year' (*sixième*) and progress up to *première* and finally *terminale*. Remember too: when writing about school, do **not** give a long list of the subjects you take!

Starter sentences

Je vais passer mes examens en mai	I'm going to sit my exams in May
J'espère réussir à mes examens	I hope to pass my exams
J'ai reçu de bonnes notes en …	I got good marks in …
Ma matière préférée, c'est le français	My favourite subject is French
Ce que je n'aime pas du tout, c'est…	What I really don't like is …
Je pense que le prof est moche	I think the teacher is awful
Je trouve que j'ai trop de devoirs	I have too much homework, I think
L'année prochaine, je vais continuer mes études au lycée	I'm going to do sixth year studies next year

Put your own phrases in the spaces below:

5 Food and drink

une baguette	a French loaf/stick
une banane	banana
du beurre	butter
un biscuit, un petit gâteau	biscuit
les bonbons (m pl)	sweets
des chips (m pl)	crisps
le chocolat	chocolate

les choux (m pl) de Bruxelles	Brussels sprouts
la confiture	jam
les escargots (m pl)	snails
du fromage	cheese
un fruit	(piece of) fruit
les fruits (m pl) de mer	sea food
du jambon	ham
un œuf	egg
du pain	bread
du porc	pork
une pomme	apple
une pomme de terre	potato
une tomate	tomato
un yaourt	yoghurt
un café	a coffee
un coca	a coke
de l'eau (f)	water
du lait	milk
de l'eau minérale	mineral water
un jus d'orange	an orange juice
un thé	a (cup of) tea
le vin	wine

Starter sentences

Mon plat favori, c'est le …	My favourite meal is …
J'adore le thé	I love tea
J'aime beaucoup les fruits	I like fruit a lot
J'aime bien les frites	I like chips
Je n'aime pas tellement le café	I don't really like coffee
Les haricots, je les déteste	I hate beans
J'ai souvent faim, l'après-midi	I'm often hungry in the afternoons
Je prends de l'eau avec mon repas	I drink water with my meals

Put your own phrases in the spaces below:

6 Family members

la famille	family
les parents (m pl)	parents
le père	father
la mère	mother
le mari	husband
la femme	wife
le frère; mon frère aîné/cadet	brother; my older/younger brother
la sœur; ma sœur aînée/cadette	sister; my older/younger sister
le fils	son
la fille	daughter
un jumeau/une jumelle	twin
le grand-père	grandfather
la grand-mère	grandmother
un petit-fils	grandson
une petite-fille	granddaughter
les petits-enfants (m pl)	grandchildren
un oncle	uncle
une tante	aunt
un cousin/une cousine	cousin
un neveu	nephew
une nièce	niece

Starter sentences

Nous sommes quatre dans ma famille	There are four of us
Je n'ai pas de frères/de sœurs	I don't have any brothers/sisters
Je suis enfant unique	I don't have any brothers or sisters

J'ai une sœur et deux frères	I have a sister and two brothers
Mon frère/Ma sœur s'appelle …	My brother/sister is called …
Mes parents s'appellent …	My parents are called …
Mes parents sont séparés/divorcés	My parents are separated/divorced
Je m'entends bien avec mes parents	I get on well with my parents
Mes parents sont très sympas	My parents are very nice
Quelquefois, je me dispute avec ma mère	I sometimes have arguments with Mum
Ma sœur est très gentille	My sister is very nice
Je peux discuter de mes problèmes avec …	I can talk about my problems with …
Je ne m'entends pas bien avec mon frère	I don't get on well with my brother
Mon frère m'énerve	My brother gets on my nerves

Put your own phrases in the spaces below:

7 The weather

la météo	the weather forecast
Quel temps fait-il?	What is the weather like?
Il fait beau tous les jours	The weather is nice every day
Il fait du soleil de temps en temps	It is sunny now and then
Il fait chaud/Il ne fait jamais chaud	It is hot/It is never hot
Il fait 25 degrés	It is 25°
Il fait souvent mauvais	The weather is often bad
Il fait froid en hiver	It is cold in winter
Il gèle pendant la nuit	It freezes over at night
Il fait du vent assez souvent	It is quite often windy
Il fait du brouillard en automne	It is foggy in autumn
Il pleut maintenant	It is raining now
Il neige en hiver	It snows in winter
Le temps est orageux	It is stormy

Seasons

le printemps	spring
l'été (m)	summer
l'automne (m)	autumn
l'hiver (m)	winter

Put your own phrases in the spaces below:

8 Hobbies and sports

Je vais au cinéma	I go to the cinema
Je vais à la pêche	I go fishing
J'écoute de la musique	I listen to music
Je lis des magazines/des livres	I read magazines/books
Je regarde la télé/des DVD	I watch TV/DVDs
Je fais du patin à glace	I go ice-skating
Je fais du roller en ligne	I go rollerblading
Je fais du cyclisme/du vélo	I go on my bike
Je fais du VTT	I go mountain-biking
Je fais du skate-board	I go boarding
Je fais de l'équitation	I go horse-riding
Je fais de la gymnastique	I do gymnastics
Je fais de la natation	I go swimming
Je fais du ski	I go skiing
Je fais du sport	I do sport
Je fais de la voile	I go sailing
Je fais des jeux vidéo	I play video games
Je joue sur l'ordinateur	I play on the computer/computer games
Je joue **de** …	I play … *(a musical instrument)*

Je joue de la guitare/du piano	I play the guitar/the piano
Je joue **à** …	I play … *(a sport)*
Je joue au basket/au foot/au tennis	I play basketball/football/tennis

Starter sentences

Il y a beaucoup de choses à faire à Glasgow	There's lots to do in Glasgow
Il n'y a rien à faire pour les jeunes	There's nothing for young people to do
Il n'y a pas beaucoup ici	There is not a lot here
Il n'y a pas de cinéma	There is no cinema
On peut aller à la maison des jeunes	You can go to the youth club
Je joue au foot tous les week-ends	I play football every weekend
Je vais au cinéma avec mes copains	I go to the cinema with my friends
Mon sport préféré, c'est le …	My favourite sport is …
Moi, j'adore jouer au tennis	I really love playing tennis
Ce que je ne supporte pas, c'est le …	What I really can't stand is …
Mardi, je joue au hockey: c'est génial!	I play hockey on Tuesdays: it's brilliant!
Je suis membre d'un club de golf	I'm in a golf club
Je suis membre de l'équipe de hockey	I'm in the hockey team

Put your own phrases in the spaces below:

9 House, daily routine and household tasks

un appartement	flat
la cave	cellar
la chambre	bedroom
la cuisine	kitchen
la douche	shower
un étage	floor (first, second, etc.)
un grenier	attic

un immeuble	block of flats
la maison	house
la salle à manger	dining room
la salle de bains	bathroom
le séjour	living room
je me réveille à …	I wake up at …
je me lève	I get up
je me lave	I get washed
je m'habille	I get dressed
je prends mon petit déjeuner	I have my breakfast
je déjeune/je dîne	I have (my) lunch/supper
je quitte la maison	I leave the house
je prends le bus	I get the bus
je rentre à la maison/chez moi	I get home
je me couche	I go to bed
je fais les courses	I do the shopping
j'aide ma mère à …	I help my mum to …
je m'occupe de mon frère	I look after my brother
je fais du baby-sitting	I babysit
je fais la cuisine	I do the cooking
je prépare le dîner	I make the tea/supper
je fais du jardinage	I work in the garden
je tonds le gazon	I cut the grass
je fais mon lit	I make my bed
je fais la vaisselle	I do the washing-up
je fais la lessive	I do the washing (clothes)
je lave la voiture	I wash the car
je mets la table	I set the table
je range/débarrasse la table	I clear the table
je passe l'aspirateur	I do the hoovering
je range ma chambre	I tidy my room
je sors la poubelle	I take out the rubbish

Starter sentences

Souvent je dois faire les courses pour ma mère	I often have to do the messages for Mum
De temps en temps, il me faut ranger ma chambre	Sometimes I have to tidy my room
Tous les jours, je fais mon lit: quelle barbe!	I make my bed every day: how boring!
Je ne fais jamais la lessive	I never do the washing

Put your own phrases in the spaces below:

10 Places in town

l'aéroport (m)	airport
un arrêt d'autobus	bus stop
la banque	bank
le bâtiment	building
la bibliothèque	library
la boîte (de nuit)	nightclub
le camping	campsite
le centre commercial	shopping centre
le centre sportif	sports complex
le château	castle
le cinéma	cinema
la cité	housing estate, city
le collège/l'école (f)	school
le commissariat/la gendarmerie	police station
l'église (f)	church
la gare	station
la gare routière	bus/coach station
un grand magasin	department store

l'hôpital (m)	hospital
l'hôtel (m) de ville	town hall
le magasin	shop
la mairie	town hall
le marché	market
la maison des jeunes	youth club
le métro	Underground
un monument	monument; tourist attraction
le musée	museum
le parc	park
la patinoire	skating rink
la piscine	swimming pool
la place	square
le pont	bridge
le port	harbour, port
la poste	post office
le stade	stadium
la station-service	petrol station
le syndicat d'initiative	tourist information office
le théâtre	theatre
la zone piétonne	pedestrian precinct

Starter sentences

À Perth, il y a beaucoup à faire et à voir!	There's lots to do and see in Perth!
Il n'y a pas grand-chose pour les jeunes	There's not a lot for young people
Chez nous, il y a une piscine	We have a swimming pool
On n'a pas de gare	We don't have a station
J'habite Dumfries depuis douze ans	I've lived in Dumfries for twelve years

Put your own phrases in the spaces below:

11 Modes of transport

en auto/en voiture	by car
en autobus	by bus
en avion	by plane
en bateau	by boat
en car	by coach
en métro	by Underground
à moto	by motorbike
à pied	on foot
en train	by train
à vélo	by bike

Starter sentences

Je vais au collège à pied, normalement	Usually I walk to school
Nous sommes allé(e)s en bus	We went by bus
Quand il pleut, je prends le bus	When it's raining, I go by bus
Je préfère aller en voiture, c'est plus vite	I prefer going by car, it's quicker
Nous sommes allé(e)s en France en train	We went to France by train
Je préfère aller à vélo, c'est plus facile	I prefer to go by bike, it's easier

Put your own phrases in the spaces below:
